T0195913

Where the Asparagus Grows

Inspirational Stories
of the cultivation of my faith

E L I Z A B E T H   B R A V O

WESTBOW
PRESS®
A DIVISION OF THOMAS NELSON
& ZONDERVAN

WestBow Press books may be ordered through booksellers or by contacting:

WestBow Press
A Division of Thomas Nelson & Zondervan
1663 Liberty Drive
Bloomington, IN 47403
www.westbowpress.com
844-714-3454

Scripture quotations marked (KJV) are taken from King James version of the Bible, public domain.

ISBN: 979-8-3850-1656-3 (sc)
ISBN: 979-8-3850-1655-6 (hc)
ISBN: 979-8-3850-1657-0 (e)

Library of Congress Control Number: 2024901062

Print information available on the last page.

WestBow Press rev. date: 02/01/2024

A Portrait of the Man Who Devoted His Life to Sowing Seeds

Who was Manuel Sarabia?

My father, Manuel Sarabia, loved tilling the ground and planting seeds bringing forth amazing plants, trees, vines, and flowers on the acre of land that God had given him. Intrigued by our beautiful yard, one day I counted the trees— pomegranate, oranges, figs, quince, apples, lemons, plums, nectarines, peaches, cherries, apricots, walnuts, olives, willow, to name a few—sixty-nine trees, all strategically placed truly creating a paradise where many sought to sit under its shade. Friends, families, church members and even strangers were able to partake in his bounty of fruits and vegetables. The grapes, sugarcane, nopales, tomatoes, and variety of berries were of the juiciest kind.

Having our own deep well producing the purest water was also a testament to my dad's ingenuity in the work he had done that many others benefited from. Ministers of great category and influence would visit with my father and partake at his table of his counsel. His great laughter would fill the room as he would share his many stories. When he would emphasize with his hands how big the fish was, I would notice how large his hands were. No matter how hard he tried, the dirt refused to be removed from his fingernails as it seemed to know of my dad's love of the earth. As the day would progress, these same men of God would find themselves sharing his favorite spot, under the apple tree by his small table toward the back of our paradise. His pastoring and mentorship went beyond the four walls of our own local church. He was much bigger than that. Many would find comfort being in his presence as he carried no agenda beyond his deep love for his God, his family, and people. He was a true man of God whose counsel impacted many prestigious men in category and thereby influenced our denomination. His words were genuine with no pretension and could be trusted. Hypocrisy was something he could never practice nor accept. In many ways, he truly was a bishop—a mentor of pastors, a true priest with a true calling. He was a leader who knew his calling, influencing twelve Sarabia ministers to answer the call to be pastors—a special calling that God placed upon our family legacy. Great men of God, such as his own younger brother, my uncle Jesus Sarabia, respected his older brother Manuel. My dad loved my uncle unconditionally and was so proud when he later became a well-known and prominent pastor with the largest congregation in Mexico in our denomination.

Raising eight children, pastoring a church while making our home a paradise took much hard work. It was his love for the earth and nature that influenced his sons to later become lovers of earth and nature themselves. Incredibly, in addition to this, my father held a full-time job as a land leveler for an Italian family in Manteca. I loved it when my mom would dress me up so pretty, hat and all, for Easter and he would take me to visit them; they had grown to love Manuel and wanted to see his little daughter. The owner's wife would look at me and tell me to put out my hand. She would then fill it up with dollar bills. I sure did love those visits! It was extremely obvious that God had truly sustained my father.

My Apa loved God, and it was this deep love, I believe, that had made my dad become such a generous man full of integrity. I witnessed many hurts my father went through, but he was one of the most forgiving people I have ever known. He never held a grudge against anyone and managed to love and appreciate despite the deep wounds that had cut into his very heart. It was this deep cry within that would reach out and touch our very own souls as he would sing his favorite songs unto the Lord. My father knew who he was and was true to himself. It was important for him to teach his sons to be men—especially men who loved God. He was anointed of God, whose oil overflowed to touch all under his influence, a man who had worked from sunup to sundown, rested in peace of God, happy and content with his relationship with his God and his family. He was also a communicator, and I loved hearing the many funny stories that would make us laugh. Even his big laughter would make us laugh. My mom's comments "Where was I? I don't remember that story" and my dad's responses to her would make us laugh. His own siblings looked up to him as the oldest of the family, as well as many nieces and nephews. Many had come and had found shelter in times of need. Whether it was the ground or in people's hearts, my father loved to sow seeds of love. (Written by Elizabeth Bravo in 2019. Thank you, Joshua, for the input you gave as I wrote this beautiful memorial to your grandpa.

Those that be planted in the house of the Lord
shall flourish in the courts of our God.
—Psalm 92:13

To my husband of thirty years, Jose Guadalupe
"Lupito" Bravo who has been my greatest inspiration
in answering God's call and going on faith

At the age of fourteen, he committed his life to serving
God. I have admired his love to sow seeds of the Gospel
in the hearts of people. Also, I am always surrounded by
beautiful plants and flowers due to his love of planting
and sowing in the ground. I love you so much.

To my firstborn son, Joshua Michael Caraballo, and our
daughter Victoria Angelica Soto. You both were baptized
during the winter, at the age of twelve, just like me. You
were planted in the house of the Lord under the pastorship
of your grandfather. You both are my miracle births.

To Bonnie, Israel, Kevin, Jacob, Susan, and our
precious grandchildren Kevin III and Yessenia.
You are all very loved. My prayer is that you
flourish in the courts of our God.

In memory of my Apa, born in Durango, Mexico. To my
Puertorriquena Mom and to my seven siblings. We were the
large Mexican–Puerto Rican family who lived on Watters Road.
All born and raised in the beautiful fertile San Joaquin Valley.

To the memory of my husband's parents,
Marcial and Saturnina Bravo
Their love for God and family has inspired the Bravo family and
many people. They raised their son, (my husband) to love God.
—Elizabeth Bravo

They shall still bring forth fruit in old age …
—Psalm 92:14

Contents

Prologue

Tears rolled down my cheeks as I drove the lonely Highway 4 toward the asparagus-packing house where my husband, Lupito, worked. Alone with my thoughts, I reflected on the past Saturday event where my father, after almost thirty years, had retired as the pastor of the church and a new pastor had been installed. The year was 1997. The church was where I had learned to sing, play the piano, and to speak and teach. Since very young, I had wholeheartedly devoted myself to helping my father. My husband and I had decided to move to another church, and I felt conflicted. I noticed the beautiful fertile fields where the asparagus grew up ahead, and I knew I would be approaching Victoria's Island. I quickly wiped away my tears and managed to put on a smile as Lupito got in the car.

The following days as I drove back and forth to Lupito's job, I continued to feel a deep heaviness in my heart. I would gaze at the beautiful sky, beyond the asparagus fields, and wonder if God had a specific purpose for my husband and me. Then one afternoon, before walking out of my home, I grabbed a writing tablet and a pen. As I began the usual journey on the lonely highway, I reached for the tablet and began writing thoughts as they came to me. First, the title "The Plan for Growth" came to me, and then the theme "Church Growth and Development." Tears flowed down my cheeks as I wrote. God was giving me an inspiration, and along with that, He was giving me hope. Good thoughts replaced the negative ones. God did have a plan for us. We just needed to weather the storm.

I was raised in the beautiful fertile valley of San Joaquin. Asparagus grew in abundance there. There is even an annual asparagus festival held in Stockton. My love of singing was watered and cultivated in the Stockton church our family attended. I was only five when the traveling children's choir I belonged to recorded an album. When I was ten, my dad became a pastor in the area. As I gave to others, God gave to me. He cultivated a seed of faith in me, and soon, like a fragile tiny blade of greenery bursting through the fertile ground, I quickly learned to look up toward the light. It was where I gained strength as I faced the harsh and unforgiving elements of the world. My first supernatural event took place on a beautiful spring day in Stockton. I was only twelve. This is where my story begins.

One

The Game of Nim

The rusty orange school bus turned onto McKinley Road, making its way toward us, the French Campers. The air felt brisk on that cool spring morning as we lined up to board the bus to Lathrop Junior High School. I saw the tall girl in front and quickly turned away, avoiding eye contact. She pointed at me and turned toward her friend. With a scornful glance, she loudly whispered, "Elizabeth's shoes are so worn out and ugly!" They burst into laughter. That girl had belittled and poked me since the third grade. It took a fight to stop the poking.

I could hear the screeching brakes of the bus as it came to a full stop. It almost ran into the overhanging branch of my favorite tree. Through the years, I watched it grow and admired its white magnolia flowers. *Someday, dear tree, I too will be strong and beautiful like you.* I looked forward to September, the month I would finally become a teenager.

I climbed onto the bus and sat in the first available seat. Unable to erase the girl's remark from my thoughts, I looked down at my shoes. They did look quite worn out. It was not easy for my parents to provide for a family of eight. Making myself comfortable for the twenty-minute trip, I took out my favorite Victoria Holt novel and spent the time reading and daydreaming that I was the beautiful Victorian heroine in the story. I paused to glance out the window at the country homes we were passing. Our unincorporated town's population was too small to justify building a junior high school. They should have counted the many sheep, goats, horses, pigs, cows, and dogs that were also raised there.

Passing the church in Lathrop where my dad pastored, I quickly put my book away and got ready to jump off. The school was just down the road. "Thank you," I uttered as I got off. I headed straight to my locker, keeping only the algebra book—my favorite subject. I noticed a group of girls were blocking my path. Taking a deep breath, I carefully made my way through. They noticed my knee-length skirt and asked me sarcastically, "Are you dressed for the '50s already? Spirit week is next week." I ignored them and quickly headed to class. It was not easy being in the spotlight due to my strict adherence to our church rules, but obedience to God and my parents was more important to me than submitting to peer pressure. Just two months earlier, I had made a commitment and was baptized.

After the Pledge of Allegiance, my math teacher, Mr. Johnston, directed our attention to the chalkboard—"Regional Annual Math Fair April 1972."

Will he pick me?

Mr. Johnston then distributed a math quiz and reminded us to keep our eyes on our own paper. As I turned in my paper, he quietly told me he had submitted my name for the math fair. A huge smile spread across my face as I thanked him and walked back to my desk. A student whispered, "He only picked you 'cause you're the teacher's pet." I ignored him and sat down, happy to be chosen.

When the day of the math fair arrived, I woke up early. April showers had been forecasted, but the sky was clear. I put on the beautiful light-blue dress Mom had laid out for me. It looked good against my light skin and hazel eyes. Apa smiled at me as I waved goodbye to Mom and got in the car. He backed out of our driveway and drove forward on Watters Road. I sat straight, not wanting to smash the curls of my light-brown medium-length hair. Five minutes later, we arrived at the meeting place. Apa gently placed his hand on my shoulder and said, "Dios te bendiga, mija." *God bless you, daughter.* My Apa and I had a special bond. Since the age of ten, I sang duets with Apa at church events. He had raised me well and would tell me, "Mija, cuida de tu testimonio." *Take care of your testimony.*

To honor him was a true pleasure for me. I felt an overwhelming peace and believed God's blessing was upon me. "Goodbye, Apa!"

I soaked in the morning's sun as I joined a few of my childhood friends and boarded the van that had just arrived. We were now on our way to the university! Arriving at the University of Pacific, my attention was drawn to the location where we were to register. The Rotunda resembled the Roman Colosseum. I had never been to Rome, but I had seen many pictures. I hoped I would survive whatever competitions I was to face! My classmates and I parted ways as we selected competitive math games. I decided to enter the classroom where the game of nim was to begin. Nim? I had never heard of that game. The description on the wall merely stated, "A game of strategy and mathematical skills."

After grabbing a pencil at the entrance, I sat next to a freckle-faced red-haired girl. She quickly crossed out a line on the practice sheet given and looked up at me impatiently, waiting for my turn. I took my cue from her and did the same. Soon, there was only one line left, and it was her turn. I told her, "Well, it looks like I won."

She said, "Of course not. The object is to be the last person to cross out the last line. You lost." She did not say it in a friendly way. It was more like a "You're not very smart" kind of a tone.

We played another game—now the real game. My competitor was more confident of her choices and made no attempt to hide her smirk as she would announce, "Your turn." I randomly crossed out any line. Soon, it was down to the last two lines, and it became clear that I had won.

One by one, every competitor who played me lost. It felt so good to be winning! I was informed that I would be continuing to the late afternoon competitions to play against last year's Nim winner. Some competitors looked at me with admiration; others just looked confused that I was beating everyone.

After a brief lunch break, I went to check out the arena where this next event would be held. Staff were busy setting up the equipment. A school administrator came over and struck up a conversation with me. The kind man was intrigued that I had won against many high schoolers. I happily answered his questions about my background. It was just small talk at first, but as our conversation ensued, I enthusiastically shared about my love for

God. Four months earlier, God had filled me with His Spirit, and today, I felt that same powerful presence. "It's inspiring to see you radiating such tranquility and confidence," he said as he left.

The time for the competitions would start any moment now. The auditorium was full. The master of ceremonies took his position behind the podium. He made a few presentations and announcements. He then called up the first top two competitors. As I watched the competitions take place, something began to happen to me. The peace and confidence I had felt left me. In its place, fear took over. I was unnerved by the fact that everyone would see my strategy—which was none.

Right then, I felt a nudge. "You're next—be ready."

My name was called. "Elizabeth Sarabia, representing Lathrop Junior High School—the game of Nim." I felt like I had solid cement shoes on. I walked up the four steps to the platform. Negative thoughts permeated my mind. *Everyone is going to see your every move. They will know you have no strategy or understanding of the game.* I took the pen offered. I did not have the skills or the strategy, and now everyone was going to know. Oh, the agony of the moment. In a matter of milliseconds, I lost. With whatever courage I could muster, I walked down the dreadful four steps and sat down.

Right then, a strong thought hit me. I had experienced the supernatural move of God's hand upon me. On my own, I never would have gotten this far in the game of nim. He had shown His favor upon me. I had been dealing with bullying and had felt unlovable. That day, I received something far greater than the second-place trophy—a strong faith. A beautiful peace settled within me as I embraced God's love.

The following Monday, at a school rally, I was honored by the school administration for being the only junior high school student in the district to bring home a trophy. I truly believed it had been God's wish for this to happen, and I felt so close to Him. I wondered if I would ever feel such a closeness again where He would show His power in my life in such a direct and supernatural way. Eight years later, it would happen again. This time, in the office of Jack Foster.

Two

Searching for the Perfect Will

Like a tree planted by rivers of water; that
brings forth fruit in its season …
—Psalm 1:3

"This Bay Area traffic is unbelievable!" I muttered as I
sped toward Sunnyvale for my job interview. The surrounding
mountains and hills looked so beautiful, reflecting such tranquility.
The traffic jams, however, filled me with stress. A few minutes
later, I exited the busy highway and made a sharp right turn onto
the parking lot of Lakeside Associates. I got off and opened the
heavy glass door of a light-gray single-story building. I noticed
the suite number on a glass window at the end of a long hallway.
There it is! Calming myself down, I slowly opened the door. The
reception area was empty. I stood there for a minute, deciding
what to do, when I heard heavy footsteps. Coming round the
corner was a serious-looking tall man.

"Good morning!" the man said as he extended his hand. "I'm Jack Foster. You must be Elizabeth?"

"Yes," I responded, shaking his hand.

"Please follow me."

I entered a large office at the end of a short hallway.

He pointed to a chair placed in front of a beautiful mahogany desk. "You're Elizabeth Sara ... Sarab ..."

I nodded as I helped him with the pronunciation of my last name. "It's kind of like *Arabia* but with an *S* in front. Sarabia."

"Thank you, Elizabeth, or do you prefer Liz?"

"Liz is fine," I replied as I smiled.

His deep voice intimidated me, but his green eyes reflected a kind spirit. "How was the traffic?" he asked as he sat down in his elegant black leather chair.

I smiled. "Well, hectic, I would say—*especially for a small-town country girl*. Your directions were easy to follow though. Thank you."

"You're welcome. Traffic here can be overwhelming. Well, Ms. Liz, you're my first interviewee this morning. Tell me about your work background."

Clearing my throat, I began sharing my work experience. I was nervous at first, but his calm demeanor helped me relax. Mr. Foster asked a few questions as he wrapped up the interview. "Thank you, Liz. Quite an impressive experience considering you're only twenty. Did you have any questions for me?"

Taking a deep breath, I decided to ask the one question that was on my mind. "Could you please tell me what type of business this is?"

Mr. Foster smiled. "Well, of course, Elizabeth. I am a rehabilitation counselor for workers' compensation cases."

As he continued to speak, I no longer listened. His answer shook me to the core. God's presence was tangible, and I struggled to sit still.

Mr. Foster noticed. "Are you OK?" he asked.

Before I could stop myself, I blurted out, "You don't understand. This job is mine! God told me about it."

Mr. Foster loosened his red tie. He appeared shaken as he stared at me. *Who was this nice young woman who had seemed so calm earlier, almost shy?*

Eight months before

I felt a great yearning within to give more of my life to planting seeds of the Gospel around the world. I had just heard the testimony of three men whose families found Christ because a missionary cared to visit their homes. *Lord, I want to do more for you!* At the time, I was working full-time, taking evening paralegal courses, and attending my Apa's church faithfully. Was this God's will for me? I wondered.

One winter morning in January, the answer came. I now knew what I needed to do. Slowly backing out of the long graveled driveway, I drove forward on Watters Road and got ready to turn right onto McKinley Avenue. I looked ahead at the train tracks and remembered how, six years earlier, my little brother and I had come close to being crushed under the wheels of a train. In the nick of time, I looked back and saw the train. We jumped to safety and avoided what could have been the end of our lives.

There was no doubt God had saved us. There was no doubt He had a will for my life.

Fifteen minutes later, I parked my car, hurried into an old five-story building, and took the elevator to the third floor. I walked into the Stockton law office where I worked and headed directly to Attorney Pat's office. "Hi Pat!" "Hi, Liz. What's the word of the Lord for me today?" Pat asked.

With a big smile, I usually would share the Gospel. Today, I was on a specific mission. "Pat, I just need to let you know that in August, I plan to quit my job here and go to Bible college." A little surprised at my seven months' notice, Pat smiled, acknowledging my statement.

Before he could say anything, I took off. "I'll be right back!" And I rushed down the stairs to the second floor. I headed to my friend Jackie's office. She was a rehabilitation counselor for workers' compensation cases. "Good morning, Jackie!"

"Hi, Liz." Her light-brown eyes were welcoming. Jackie was older, and I loved her counseling. She was such a peaceful, kind woman. She motioned for me to sit.

"I need to get back to work, Jackie, but I couldn't wait to tell you."

"Sure, what is it, Liz?" she asked politely.

"I'll be moving to San Jose to go to Bible college in August!"

She smiled. Jackie knew my father was a pastor and my life revolved around the church. "How exciting, Liz. Listen, be sure to come and see me before you move. I can connect you with a part-time job there in my same line of business. They pay well, Liz."

"Thank you, Jackie. I better get back to my office. Have a good day!" I said as I headed out and walked back up the stairs to start my workday.

Time flew as I devoted myself to my church, my job, and my education. Spring was ending, and Bible college enrollment was around the corner. *Well, I better let Apa know of my decision.* I knew Mom would be fine, but I was concerned about Apa. I saw him sitting alone at our kitchen table. *Now's a good time,* I thought as I pulled out the chair and sat down. "Apa, you want a piece of cake?" I asked.

"Si, gracias, mija."

Serving him the delicious slice of Mom's famous homemade cheesecake with a hot cup of black coffee, I sat across from him. I sat there watching him add the cream and sugar. "Apa?"

He looked up. "Si, hija?"

"With your permission, in August, I plan to move to San Jose to go to Bible college." Apa slowly took a drink and quietly looked at me. How many times had this kitchen table witnessed the debates between him and his daughter? She was a debater, that's for sure, and a smart one at that.

"No, mija ..." *The dreaded no!* "Why you wanna go anyway?" he continued. "La mayoria son hombres que van. The majority who attend are male. It maka no sense why you quit tu trabajo [your job] to go to that college."

"Why not, Apa? Please let me go, please." I begged. Apa was adamant that he would not give me permission.

Feeling defeated, I got up and went to my bedroom. *I'll continue tomorrow. He's probably too tired to listen.* The following week, I continued pleading, but to no avail. Because I would not leave without his blessing, I decided to quash the desire to go to college. *Obviously, it must have not been God's will.*

Ironically, that same week, my employer's lucrative five-year county contract expired, and for the first time in many years, a competitor outbid them for the contract. In a matter of two short weeks, the law firm was dissolved. The partnership decided to pursue only civil cases, and we moved out of the five-story building into a smaller place. I was grateful that they decided to keep me employed until I could find a new job.

I applied for a position with the county, and in July, I was offered a job as the San Joaquin County chief jailer's secretary. I shared the good news with Attorney Pat. "I just need to pass the physical next week." *Perhaps this was God's will for me all along.*

That weekend, I drove to the Santa Cruz Mountains, where I was a counselor at a church camp. I was settling into the small cabin when I heard a knock. "Betty?"

"Yes?"

"Your mom called."

"OK, thank you," I replied. All my church friends and family knew me as Betty. Mom always said that in Puerto Rico, the Elizabeths are called Bettys. Concerned, I quickly returned her call, wondering why she had called me. "Betty, the chief jailer is trying to get ahold of you. He didn't say why. Here's the number," she said.

"OK, thanks, Mom." *What could be the urgency?* I wondered as I dialed his number.

"Hello, Elizabeth. Thank you for returning my call. I'm so sorry but ..." ... *I'm so sorry? Oh no!*

He continued, "I'm so sorry but I cannot offer you the position. My secretary has returned. She did not like working for the post office after all." *What's wrong with the post office? That's not fair!* Many thoughts came to my mind, but instead, I merely thanked him and hung up. I stood there stunned, looking at the old, discolored phone booth. *Perhaps it was not God's will after all.*

I then deliberately pushed the negative thought aside, grateful for the wonderful weekend ahead. Instead, I soaked in the scents of the sweet aroma of nature, the breathtaking beauty of the rugged mountains, the tall, majestic pine trees, the small wooden cabins, and the angelic sounds of the singing birds and the laughing children.

As soon as I returned to work on Monday, I updated Pat on my job status. "How can they do that!?" he asked.

"I know—makes no sense," I replied.

Later that day, Pat gave me a phone number to call. "Call them. They're my friends, and they're looking for a criminal legal secretary. It's a great opportunity, Liz."

Two weeks later, I walked into the office of a prestigious law firm for an interview. Attorney Pat had given them an excellent reference. I was nervous, but I felt that the interview went well. That following morning, I received a call offering me the position. My start date was to be September 15. I felt relieved. *Perhaps this was God's will for my life all along.*

That next Sunday, I noticed a Bible college recruiter entering our church. I later overheard him explaining the campus safety rules to my Apa. *Why bother?* I thought. *I'm not going anyhow.*

That same night, when we arrived home, Apa looked at me and told me I could go if I still wanted to. I didn't respond as we both knew it was too late. I had made no preparations.

The following day, I noticed Pat heading in my direction. He seemed bothered. "Hey, Liz. I was just wondering. Back in January, you mentioned about going to Bible college. What happened? You never talked about it anymore."

I looked into the sky-blue eyes of the tall blond-haired man, wondering if I had just heard him correctly. *Why in the world was he bringing this up now? He knew that I already had found a job. Something or someone must have triggered his memory.* "Funny you ask now, Pat. The truth is my dad was against it from the beginning. Yesterday, however, he said he had reconsidered. It's too late now though. I'm not able to fully cover the deposit or any costs involved. I'm not prepared, and I needed at least to find a part-time job."

At that moment, Pat said, "Keep the faith, Liz. Keep the faith." *Keep the faith? What had gotten into Pat?* "By the way, Liz, how much is the cost to attend for a year?"

"I honestly don't know, Pat, but I can look into it."

"Yes, Liz, please do that for me, and remember, keep the faith."

That evening, I was able to find out the costs involved, and the following morning, I gave Pat the information.

Pat thanked me, and said, "Keep the faith, Liz." He turned and walked to his office.

It was now almost the end of my workday, and I noticed Pat hurrying to my desk. Pat smiled as he handed me an envelope. "Liz, I have something for you." He waited for me to open the envelope. I couldn't believe my eyes! "My wife and I would like to pay a year's expenses for Bible college."

What? The amount of the check would cover room and board, a year's tuition, meals, and even my books. It was six times my monthly salary. *First the visiting minister, then my Apa, and now this?* Unable to contain the tears that now trickled down my cheeks, I thanked Pat. I believed God had touched his heart. *This had to have been God's perfect will for me all along!*

Running through the front door of my house that day after work, I excitedly called out to my mom. I saw her standing by the kitchen sink. She turned and looked at me with her beautiful hazel-green eyes. *Boy, my mom is pretty.* I thought as I approached her. Mom was only 5'2" but she looked taller. She always had good posture and loved wearing high heels. I showed her the check and explained what had happened. Taken aback at first, my mom just smiled. She herself had had many experiences where God answered her prayers. "Where's Apa?"

"Esta mero atraz," Mom said. "He's way in the back." Mom made it a point to talk in Spanish to all eight of us. She wanted to make sure we would at least understand it even if we struggled speaking it."

"OK, thanks, Mom!" Apa already said I could go to Bible college this past Sunday! I was so excited with renewed hope. Yes, it must have been God's will! *Yes, there he is—way in the back like Mom said.* How I loved my Apa. I knew that being his first daughter after having three sons was such a joy to my Apa's heart, and his tendency to be overprotective could be understood.

Apa looked up, trying to figure out what message his Betty could have now. She was only ten when he was called to pastor, and she had fully devoted herself to the church, singing, teaching, and even learning to play piano when the need arose for a pianist.

In her teen years, there had been many tumultuous moments where her questionings had exasperated him, but there was no doubt of her love for God. The sound of his daughter's happy voice interrupted his thoughts. "Apa, look what I have! It's a check, Apa, to pay for college in full for the year!"

Apa did not say a word. Our eyes met. "Mija, I haven't given you permission to go to college."

Huh? Didn't Apa say he was giving me permission? Frowning, I quickly turned and ran back to the house. I refused to accept Apa's disapproval, and I had no plans to argue with him. *Please, God, I need your direction!* I hid myself in a private corner of our living room and began to pray. I got out my pink Bible. "OK, God, please talk to me. I need to know if it is Your will for me to go to Bible college or not." I randomly opened my Bible.

I looked at the first verses my eyes fell upon, Hebrews 10:35–36. "Cast not away therefore your confidence, which hath great recompense of reward. For ye have need of patience, that after ye have done the will of God, ye might receive the promise." How perfect!

Wanting further reassurance, I called Ruth. I had known Ruth for many years. Like me, she was a pastor's daughter. She was older than me, was married, and had children. Many people knew of her fervent prayer life and her great faith in God and came to her for counsel. "Ruth? It's me, Betty."

After I shared my dilemma, Ruth briefly prayed over me. "Betty, God has just given me a verse for you. Do you have your Bible?"

"Yes, Ruth, I do. I was just reading it."

"OK. Turn to Hebrews"

"Hebrews?"

"Yes, Hebrews 10:35–36."

"Ruth!" I exclaimed. "Those were the verses God had just given me before calling you right now!" At that moment, we both began uplifting our voices in worship and praise as God's presence filled the room.

Ruth's last words were "Betty, you know what you need to do. God has spoken. He has given you His approval and blessing." *No longer was there any doubt in me as to God's perfect will. I had found His perfect will for me.*

Hanging up the phone, I ran back to look for Apa. He was bent over, watering his bounty of plants and trees whose fruit had blessed many throughout our eighteen years of living there. "Apa!" Apa looked up. I once again reiterated to my Apa all that had happened that day and confirmed that I would be going to Bible college. My father, seeing my spiritual connection in this, finally resolved to give me his blessing.

The following week, I drove to the Bible college in San Jose and happily registered for classes and handed staff the check. That check was a blessing to the school as they had been struggling financially. It was an answered prayer. After settling into my dorm, I drove to the neighborhood store The Pink Elephant and bought the *San Jose Mercury* newspaper. I now needed to find a part-time job. The classifieds section was at least five pages, and it was overwhelming to me as I was not familiar with all the Bay Area cities listed on the pages. I was drawn to a very small ad, "Part-time bilingual secretary position," and decided to call the number listed. A man answered and scheduled me for an interview. The business was called Lakeside Associates.

God had led me to this moment where I now sat in front of the interviewer. I had just lost control. The interviewer Jack was a workers' compensation rehabilitation counselor, the same position as my Stockton friend Jackie had! Even their names were alike. I could hear her prophetic words, "Be sure you see me before you leave, Liz. I can connect you with a part-time job working for a workers' compensation rehabilitation counselor." I never had a chance to connect with Jackie before leaving.

Mr. Foster responded to my outburst in a serious low tone. "You're not the only applicant. There are others and they are also very qualified. I will let you know no sooner than Friday."

"Thank you!" I said as I did my best to bottle in all my emotions and quietly walked out. I was so overwhelmed by God's power.

That evening at church, the preacher asked if anyone in the congregation wanted to give thanks. "Yes," I said, trying not to yell. "I want to thank God for the job He gave me today." I was the happiest girl that day. It wasn't because I had a job; it was because I had witnessed the hand of God move on my life. The following morning, Thursday, Jack called to offer me the job. He couldn't even wait till Friday. It came as no surprise to me.

There was no doubt that attending Bible college had been God's will for my life. I learned about Bible theology, formed new friendships, and learned to handle the dorm life, among other things. I was away from my comfort zone, and I relied on God a lot. He granted my desires, even small, insignificant ones, and I felt as though He favored me. My relationship with God deepened, and my faith in Him increased day by day. Nine months went quickly by, and soon it was time to return home. I said my goodbyes to my new friends and headed back to French Camp. I wondered what lay ahead. Surely, God would continue to bless me. My faith was stronger than ever. Never did I dream what lay ahead. I would be entering a valley so dark and so lonely. I would find myself sinking so deep into the mire that I almost lost my will to live.

Three

Conqueror of Dragons ... or Not?

Save me, O God, for the waters are come in unto my
soul. I sink in deep mire, where there is no standing; I am
come into deep waters, where the floods overflow me.
—Psalm 69:1

One Sunday evening, as I played the grand piano and sang
for our small congregation, I noticed a handsome man had walked
in. He looked my way with his black almond-shaped eyes, causing
me to quickly look away. After church, I overheard him say he
was visiting from Puerto Rico. I extended my hand to the lean,
muscular dark man and welcomed him. "Mi nombre es Betty."

"Hola." He told me his name and shared that his parents had
named him after a German legendary hero who conquered a
dragon.

Interesting, I thought, *a conqueror of dragons—with a sense of humor.
I like it.*

One day, a friend hinted that the man was interested in me. "In me?"

She nodded. "Yes, he's got his eye on you. You just don't see it." I kept silent, but I wondered if it was true. Our friendship was certainly blooming. One evening, as our youth group was about to enter our favorite restaurant, we noticed an old man selling some beautiful paintings. My new friend stopped and asked me, "Cual te gusta?" *Which painting do you like?* I pointed to a sunset view one. He turned to the man and pointed to the picture. "Quiero ese." *I want that one.* He turned around and gave it to me. I thanked him as I shyly accepted the expensive gift.

Five months later, he proposed to me. Although I felt our relationship was moving very fast, I said, yes! After all, wasn't it about time? My mom was seventeen when she got married, and I was already twenty-two years old! I had fallen in love. I vividly remembered the day he arrived at my home in French Camp. He was there to ask my Apa for his blessing. We felt great joy when Apa gave it. The following day, however, I felt a tiny bit of fear when Apa approached me. He looked serious. We were alone. He said, "Yo se que el es buen parecido, mija, pero no lo hagas por esa razon." *I know he is good-looking, daughter, but don't do it for that reason.* That was the only time he voiced his concern over our engagement. I reassured my Apa that he was the one. Perhaps my dad was just being overprotective.

The wedding date was rapidly approaching. Eight months had gone by. One week before the wedding, I got a call from my brother. "Betty, can you come over? I would like to talk to you." I rushed over to their home. "Have a seat, Betty." He continued, "Do you remember Margaret Garcia?"

"Yes?" I replied.

"Well, I don't know if you know this, but a week before her wedding, she called it off. She realized that he was not the one for her."

"Oh. OK?" I replied.

"Well, I feel you should call off the wedding. We do not feel he is the one for you. He's nice, but he's not for you."

I listened quietly. I had always admired my brother. "No!" I angrily replied. "You guys are judging him way too harshly." Deep down, however, my brother's words bothered me. There were red flags I had chosen to ignore. I recalled the day we argued over rumors of him and a promiscuous lady. I had caught him in some lies. That evening, when I confronted him, he had an anxiety attack. I broke off the engagement. The next day, he begged me to forgive him. I believed his explanations and our engagement was back on. *It's my own insecurity that's causing our arguments,* I reasoned. *Our love will conquer everything.*

On a warm day in August, surrounded by my friends and family, I walked down the aisle of a beautiful church. Although only 5'4", I felt almost as tall that day as my Apa, donning my expensive pearl high-heeled shoes. I felt beautiful in my size 9 white lace-trimmed wedding gown as I smiled beneath the veil, at my family and childhood friends who were in attendance. "Who gives this woman to be married?"

My dear Apa answered, in a low and serious tone, "I do." With tears in his eyes, my Apa hugged me and left to sit next to my beautiful mom. As I stood at the sacred altar next to my future husband, my every concern melted away as we shared our personal vows to each other, before God and men.

Seven months later, we traveled to Puerto Rico to meet my husband's family. One morning, as we walked into the neighborhood where he had been raised, he pointed to a quaint home with a beautiful large porch, surrounded by tropical plants. It was the home of his ex-girlfriend. As we continued to walk in silence, I tried to quash my feelings of insecurity. Did he marry me on a rebound? Later that day, as we walked into a store, he picked up and smelled the Tabu perfume on the counter. I later learned it was her favorite perfume. He never knew mine. It was clear that my husband had given up a lot when he moved to California. His friends, family, culture, musical band, and his beloved pastor were all tied to this pearl of an island.

Saying our goodbyes, we boarded the plane in San Juan, Puerto Rico. I looked over at the man sitting beside me, and I could see a faraway look in his eye. Was it regret that I saw? All the fanfare of the courtship, the wedding, and the honeymoon was over, and the reality of our married lives now lay before us. I buried negative thoughts that were beginning to infiltrate my thoughts. I was letting my imagination take over, and there was no truth to it. He loved me. Didn't he? Our path would soon take a sharp turn. Torrential rains and violent windstorms were coming. Chaos and destruction lay ahead. It was just a matter of time.

When we returned home, I found out I was pregnant. I felt joy in my soul and looked forward to the day I would hold my baby in my arms. I loved the fact that the baby was due on my father's birthday, November 15. I did, however, notice a great change in my husband's behavior after returning from Puerto Rico, and we had many arguments—mostly due to my lack of trust in him. We did our best to work matters out as I now had a child within.

Most of the time, I would choose to believe his many excuses and apologize for not believing him in the first place.

One day, my Apa asked my husband to prepare to preach on our fasting day on October 7. My Apa loved mentoring young people and often gave them opportunities to develop their God-given gifts and talents. My husband replied joyfully to Apa, "Voy a predicar de Josue, mi favorito de la Biblia!" I will preach about Joshua, my favorite in the Bible. The days leading up to October 7 were very peaceful days in our home. It made me so happy to see my husband devote his time to preparing his sermon. He seemed happy, and we both looked forward to that special day.

When the day arrived, however, instead of going to church, we rushed that morning to St. Joseph's hospital in Stockton. At 5:55 p.m., our baby was born. A son! He weighed only 4 lbs. 18 oz. We named him Joshua after the preaching title. He was beautiful with abundant hair and green eyes. As I weakly lay on the hospital bed, I asked for my little sister to come in. "He's so tiny!" Margarita said.

"Yes, he is," I replied. "Do you want to give him his middle name?" I asked as I looked into her beautiful blue eyes.

She responded, "Well, I do like Michael Jackson. How about Michael?"

"Joshua Michael … yes! A beautiful name." Yes! A beautiful name, his father agreed. Since Joshua had come over a month early, our home was not prepared to receive him. After a week's stay in the hospital, we were both ready to go home.

I was amazed at the beautiful blue nursery room that my husband had prepared for his son.

Sadly, in the months that followed, I noticed a drastic change in my husband. He lost his desire to attend church with me, and our arguments increased. Every argument seemed to give him an opportunity to leave for hours at a time. When Joshua Michael was only nine months old, my husband stormed out of the house, yelling, "It's over!" He didn't return that night. Desperate, I called an aunt in Tracy to talk to him. Usually, that was where he would go. She coldly informed me that he had flown to Puerto Rico that morning. "Puerto Rico?"

"Si, su mama le dio su boleto." *His mom gave him her ticket.* I immediately called his home in Puerto Rico.

His mom answered. "Porque quedarse en un matrimonio donde solo hay argumentos?" *Why stay in a marriage where there're constant arguments?* she demanded. I didn't respond.

My husband then got on the line and asked, "Que quieres? No puedo vivir contigo. Siempre peleando. Especialmente, rodeado de tu familia—juzgandome." *What do you want? I can't live with you. Always fighting. Especially, surrounded by your family, judging me.*

"How about if we move away and start over?" I begged. He stood quiet and then replied that if I could find a place far away, he would consider returning, but only then.

Hanging up, I looked over at my little Joshua trying to get out of his stroller. My heart hurt so much. *My poor innocent child. Perhaps it was my insecurities and jealousy that had pushed his father away.* My only hope now was to find that faraway place. *Who can help us?* Then, a thought came. *Maybe Pastor Juan?* Our family had met him on our visits to my grandparents down South. I called him and reluctantly shared the situation.

He was pensive for a while, and then quietly responded, "I can help. Tell him he has a home and a job here." I immediately called and told him what the pastor had said. He agreed to return. He flew directly to San Diego, where the pastor received him. The pastor took him under his wing and helped him. His family and church welcomed us. The move was good for our marriage.

One day, something happened that would change the course of our lives. When I picked up my son after work, I noticed he had a fever. *Why didn't his babysitter call me?* I buckled him in, anxious to get home, where I could tend to him. He appeared lethargic. I stopped at a stop sign and glanced back. Joshua was convulsing! His eyes had rolled back, and his helpless body was having uncontrollable jerks! Stopping in the middle of the street, I got off and ran to get him. Carrying my little child, I ran through the neighborhood, knocking at doors, praying for help. Someone open the door, please! Finally, an older lady answered. "Oh, my! Come in, come in! She said as she dialed 911. The ambulance rushed my little one to the hospital. Sometime later, the doctor called me in. He showed me Joshua's X-rays, pointing to some cells. "Your son has meningitis. If it had been bacterial, it could have been fatal. But it's viral meningitis. With medication, he will get better." That evening, we both fell on our knees and gave thanks to God for our son.

Believing our marriage was now healed, we decided to move back to Stockton, where Mom could watch our son. I was reinstated to the City of Stockton position as the fire marshal's secretary.

At first, it appeared that everything was good between my husband and me. This soon changed, however, when he got a job out of town. On certain days, he would not return home until the next day. Of course, this only led to arguments. He lost all interest in attending church with me and our son.

A week before Joshua's third birthday, my husband and I had a huge argument. He slammed the door as he walked out. Full of despair, I walked in circles, yelling my frustrations over and over. It was the first time I had ever said a curse word. I was so overcome with emotion that I hadn't even noticed little Joshua following me. He was stomping his little feet, marching behind me, muttering the same swear words. I couldn't believe it! It brought me back to my senses. *What was I doing to my precious son?*

In January of 1988, my husband had a change of heart and expressed his wish to get back together. He suggested we spend the upcoming Valentine's weekend together. I felt renewed hope. Maybe it helped that I no longer pressured him to be a husband, a father, a Christian, or a provider.

In February, we drove out of town to Carson City, Nevada. That evening, as we got dressed to go out to dinner, a note fell out of his wallet. He didn't notice, so I quickly picked it up and saw a Tracy address neatly printed on it. I quickly put it in my purse.

We had a wonderful weekend together, and soon it was over. He dropped me off and rushed back to Tracy. *Why the hurry?* I wondered. I pulled out the note hidden in my purse and looked at it again. "I wonder whose address is this?"

The next weekend, I said to Joshua. "Let's get you dressed, Bunchie. We're going to see Papa." Once in Tracy, I pulled out the note. I knew it wasn't his aunt's home. I looked at the address again and quickly found Sixth Street. I turned in the street and drove slowly, looking for the block number. *It must be that apartment complex ahead.* Cautiously driving forward, I quickly stopped when I noticed a familiar small white truck parked in the middle of the street in front of the complex. The truck was facing in my direction, but I somehow managed to quickly pull aside before being noticed. I was able to see from afar and noticed a man sitting in the driver's seat. It was my husband! My heart jumped a beat. "No, God! No!"

An attractive woman quickly jumped into the vehicle. She leaned over and kissed him. I winced inside. The pain was deep. *Please, God, help me.* She was the reason for his many visits to Tracy. How could I have been so blind? He drove off and literally passed our car on that wide street and didn't even notice us. His eyes were only for her. Thankfully, Bunchie was playing with his favorite stuffed animal, Roger Rabbit. Somehow, I controlled my emotions, as I quickly made a U-turn, determined to follow him. He was heading toward his aunt's home. Once there, he parked across the street. I quickly parked the next block over and sat in my car.

When I saw him get out of the truck, I got off and watched him from afar. He spotted me and ran toward me. He yelled, "Que haces aqui! Vete!" *What are you doing here? Leave!* His girlfriend had gotten off the truck and saw me.

In anger, I yelled, "He's my husband!"

Seeing I was determined to stay there, my husband turned and headed back to calm his girlfriend down. I grabbed Joshua, who had managed to get out of the car. At that moment, my husband fell on the sidewalk. It appeared he was having an anxiety attack. His girlfriend and family rushed to his side to help him. I noticed how familiar the family was with his girlfriend. *How long had this affair been going on?* I wondered. The recent attempt at reconciliation was a complete lie. Everyone entered the aunt's home. Just before closing her door, the aunt signaled with her hand for us to come in. I then walked in with Joshua, and we both quickly sat down in a corner of her large living room.

Once inside, I noticed the girlfriend whispering to my husband, "Tell her. Tell her." She then got up and moved away. My husband motioned for me to come. He was lying down on a cot. I walked over to him and sat down. Pointing to his girlfriend, he coldly said, "I don't love you anymore. Yo amo a ella." *I love her.*

Those words tore into me. I felt totally crushed. I called out to Joshua, who was playing with toys in another room. "Joshua, *mijo*, let's go home now." I grabbed his little hands, and with my head held up high, I walked out, anxious to get home. As soon as I was in the safety of my car, my volcano of emotions erupted. I let out a bloodcurdling scream. *Why, Lord? Why? I have never left from serving you since I was a child. Why?*

I continued to drive. A few minutes later, a police officer stopped me, but I didn't care as my life was over. As the tall thin officer approached the yellow Ford Fairmont car, he stood and looked at me. He gave me a moment to control my weeping. My words came storming out, "I'm sorry, officer."

He waited for me to gain control and noticed the innocent child sitting quietly in his car seat. The officer smiled at him. My little boy smiled back, but his eyes looked sad. Tears were trickling down his puffy cheeks. The officer gently said, "Do you know why I stopped you?"

"No, officer, I don't."

"You didn't stop at the sign."

"Oh, I'm … so sorry, officer. I didn't see it."

"Listen, up ahead there's a café. Why don't you stop there and maybe drink a cup of coffee to calm your nerves? It is dangerous to drive in your condition. I won't give you a ticket. Please be safe." In between the heavy sobs, I thanked the officer and slowly pulled back onto the street.

As the months passed by, I got deeper into depression. I struggled to cope with life. Had the dragon finally won? The wellspring of songs that had been in me since very young no longer sprang forth. Instead, grief overwhelmed my spirit. Waking up to face another sunrise was a struggle that I longed to end. The pain was deep; my soul only wept. On one of my darkest moments, I considered ending my life. Crouched inside my pitch-black closet, I looked down at the small knife I was holding.

"Forever in Its Time"

Forever in its time, forever in its
time, forever in its time.
Lying here in a pool of tears. So
many problems, so many fears,
The life I live is crashing,
crashing before my eyes.
There is no one to hear me, to
hear my lonely cries.

My life is full of darkness, silence all around,
Nothing more, nothing less, except
the chains that keep me bound.
I am surely dying a slow and fateful death,
I am surely dying with every painful breath,
But not a death that one would think;
it's a death within the mind.
One that traps you in eternity forever in its time.
Forever in its time, forever in its
time, forever in its time …
—Joshua Michael Caraballo

I should just slit my wrists and end my life. Sobbing and contemplating death, I sat in complete silence. At that moment, a song began to play on my bedroom radio. *Who turned it on? I was totally alone.* The song touched my soul. I got out of the closet and sat in the corner of my bed. With tears gushing down my face, I soaked in God's love as He consoled my grieving spirit through the beautiful song. At that very moment, a thought entered my mind. *Go to your childhood church.*

That next day, I and little Joshua attended Stockton church. It was painful to be around people, but I forced myself to stay. The hymns, God's word, and love from the congregants and leaders there were bringing healing to my broken heart. The months went by, and the marriage was officially over. I found it almost impossible to sing anymore as grief had overcome my soul.

One day, I was busy cleaning my parents' living room, when out of the blue I began singing. The song was called "Cuando llegue el final" (When the end comes).

My Apa overheard me. He felt such joy when he heard me that he walked over to my mom and whispered, "Me da mucho gusto oir Betty cantar. Va estar bien." (I am so happy to hear Betty singing. She's going to be fine.)

I didn't realize until then the pain my Apa had been holding within because of me. My song had finally returned, and Apa was right; not only would I be fine, but God had prepared a new path for me.

Four

He Restores My Soul

"...Rooted ... in love."
—Ephesians 3:17

I could see the light as I gradually edged myself out of the dark tunnel. Although God had removed all reservoirs of sadness, I felt restless. It had been four years since the divorce, and I struggled to find God's purpose for me.

In January 1993, I attended a special church event in Stockton. God already had mapped out a plan for me, but I didn't know it. When I walked in, I noticed a distinguished-looking older gentleman sitting toward the back. His black straight hair was neatly trimmed and combed in place. I noticed his western outfit. *He sure could pass for a Western movie star. All he needs is a cowboy hat.* The suit fit him perfectly, accenting his broad shoulders and slim physique. His crisp white shirt complemented his medium-brown complexion.

I was glad to see my friends from the neighboring churches, and we had a wonderful time worshipping God in unison. As soon as we said a prayer of dismissal, I noticed the handsome man walking toward me. He looked familiar. It was Lupito Bravo, the oldest brother of a close family friend. Since a very young man, he had devoted his life to church ministry. Although I was aware that he had faced certain setbacks, I always held him in high esteem.

"Praise the Lord. How are you?" Lupito said as he offered me a pen. His captivating reflective eyes accented by dark eyelashes drew me in.

"I'm fine, thank you." I looked at the pen. "This is from your brother's business. I want one with your name," I teased. He smiled. As we stood at the altar of the church, we briefly gazed into each other's eyes. I quickly turned away and made an excuse to leave. As I drove home, I thought about him and hoped that our paths would cross again.

That next day, as I played the grand piano at my church, Lupito walked in. He was our visiting preacher for our evening service! From that day forward, Lupito began visiting our church. The courtship began rather quickly. It became evident that we were destined to be together, and we believed God had a hand in this. The love and tenderness he showed me seemed authentic. God had brought my soul mate, and God now had a vessel to do His great work through us as we became one. Eleven months later, on November 20 at 2:00 p.m., we exchanged our vows in the presence of God, our family and friends, and three witnesses who stood before us—my brother minister Manuel Sarabia Jr., my brother-in-law Pastor Roy Bravo, and my cousin Pastor Alberto Sarabia. We were joined together at the very altar in Stockton where we had spoken our first words to each other. At the very church where God had restored me from the deep sadness I had faced just a few years prior, we held hands as I sang "Whither thou goeth, I will go" to my husband. I was thirty-four and he forty-seven.

Two years later, God blessed my womb again, and on September 10, Victoria Angelica was born in Stockton at full term. Her tiny head was covered by an amazing veil of shiny black velvet hair. It had been eleven years since I held a newborn in my arms. I had already experienced three miscarriages, and I wondered if I was now barren. As I looked into the adoring eyes of my precious daughter, I felt great peace and joy. Everything seemed to be going so well. Never did I imagine that two years later, our comfort zone would be shaken, and a life-changing decision would be made. The song I had sung at our wedding was now to be tested.

Five

The Call of the Master

Preach the word, be ready in season and out of season …
—2 Timothy 4:2

My parents have taught me since I was little to try
to find out what His will is and to follow it. To
my parents, His will was to move from Stockton,
where I was born, and evangelize. It was very
hard for me because we would be moving all the

time, but that shaped who I am today and taught
me to learn how to make friends wherever I go.

—Victoria

I pondered the decision that I was about to make. "Is this really you, Lord? My son was thirteen and my daughter two. Did they not need the stability and the security my job had given them? "Lord, what is Your will for us?" we cried out one day as my husband Lupito and I sat in the living room of our French Camp home. Desperate for an answer, I opened the Bible, to Matthew 9:37–38. "Pray to the Lord of the harvest … for the field is great but the laborers are few." Saying no was no longer an option. God had spoken. The trials we were going through and the true stories we were listening to ("Goodbye is not forever," "Three months under the snow," "Abraham and Sarah") had pricked our hearts.

Lupito dropped me off at work and continued toward the Landmark Christian Men's Conference three blocks away. "Bye, hon, maybe I'll see you later!" I yelled out as I walked into the Wells Fargo building where the City Housing Department leased the second floor. Seventeen years, God had blessed me in my career with the City of Stockton.

"Hi, Liz!" Brenda cheerfully said as she stood up and looked over at me from her office cubicle. "Why are you so quiet today? Are you OK?"

I smiled at Brenda. "Good, thanks!" I replied and quickly got busy responding to the pending inbox messages. As I worked on an agenda report, I couldn't shake off a recurring thought that overpowered my mind. I got up and briefly whispered a prayer as I walked over to my supervisor's office. *OK, Lord. I will do it. This is the day. This is the moment.*

I could see the older elegant woman on the phone. Stacey was a good supervisor. "Stacey?"

"Yes, Liz?"

"I need to run over to connect with my husband. He's downtown at a Landmark Men's Conference." In response to her question, I quickly explained why it was called Landmark. Thanking her, I quickly headed toward the exit, passing by receptionist Debbie's cubicle.

"How's my boy?" Debbie asked, pointing to my son Joshua's picture. She had watched him mature into a teenager. With a thumbs-up, I smiled as I hurriedly walked out the glass door.

"Boy, it's cold today!" I exclaimed as I pulled my sweater tightly around me. *I should have put my jacket on.* I headed north. As I passed the City Hall building with the huge pillars, I recalled the day I lost my footing there and fell ten steps. I was more embarrassed than hurt. I continued walking, trying to erase the fears I had about being uprooted out of the fertile valley where I had lived for the last thirty-eight years of my life. *There it is!* I entered the building where the suited men were all gathered that morning. I paused. What I was about to do would change our lives forever.

"Praise the Lord," I said to the usher, trying not to sound anxious. My voice echoed in the empty foyer. Lowering my voice, I continued, "My husband is in there," pointing to the closed doors. "Could you please get him for me?"

"Praise the Lord, sister! Of course, I'll go find him."

I described my husband, hoping he would find him soon. A few minutes later, I saw Lupito.

"Hi, hon, are you OK?" he anxiously asked me.

"Hon," I calmly replied, "I can't hold it off any longer … I'm going to submit my letter of resignation." I waited for his reaction.

Tears filled his eyes as he nodded his head. "Yes. We must obey. I can't wait to share with you what just happened." He paused a moment to wipe his eyes. Lupito continued, "A missionary spoke about hardships and blessings he and his family had when they obeyed God's call to the mission field. He said it was worth it all.

"What really touched me," Lupito continued, "was when the missionary became silent—almost as though God had spoken to him and then he pointed straight toward me and said, 'And you—what are you going to do about it?'" Lupito and I were overwhelmed how God had just confirmed the decision we were about to make.

I gently touched his arm. "Hon, I need to hurry back. Love you!" I felt no worries about our future as I knew we were in God's hands.

I typed up the letter of resignation. The Lord had impressed upon my heart to give them a maximum of two weeks' notice, not one day more. It landed on February 11. Ironically, many times the numbers 2 11 or 11 11 would later represent a sign of God's involvement in our lives. I handed my resignation to my supervisor. "What's this, Liz?" she said as she read it. "Are you sure, Liz?" It was a top management position that paid extremely well. "I feel this has something to do with that Landmark." She smiled. "Can your last day be on Friday instead of Wednesday?"

I apologized and told her I could not go beyond the two weeks.

We moved into a fifth-wheel trailer to temporarily live until the Lord would lead us to our new home. The fifth wheel was

very nice. We could cordon off the upper living-room section, and Joshua, our teenager, could have his own space. Since ministry has always been in our hearts, we accepted the invitation to travel to Texas to minister in the churches there. I took advantage of the trip and accepted the opportunity to record a new CD in Arizona. We felt blessed when Alex Spanos, owner of the San

Diego Chargers, felt moved to send a $1,000 check toward our ministry.

When we arrived in Donna, Texas, our friend welcomed us. "I have churches lined up that are waiting for

you both to minister. Where's your son?" Bishop Andy asked. "These next three days, our youth group will be selling fireworks. I'm sure Josh would like to be with them."

"Well, Bishop," my husband responded, "he stayed in our fifth-wheel trailer at the RV park."

"Do you think he'll talk to the youth pastor?" Bishop asked.

Lupito replied, "It's worth a try. He won't listen to us, but maybe someone else."

"OK, what trailer park? I'll send him right away." Half an hour later, we saw Joshua sitting in the youth pastor's car driving into the church parking lot. We later saw that Joshua was laughing with the group as he sold fireworks. We smiled at the pastor, feeling so relieved at the change in attitude. Ministering those next two weeks in Texas was amazing! Having our son finally feel happy with his new friends in Texas gave us peace.

The Lord allowed us to minister to the congregations of Dallas, Garland, Fort Worth, Donna, Pharr, Elsa, Mission, and McAllen. Lupito even baptized distant cousins of the famous singer Julio Iglesias. The Texan people embraced us with such love. Finishing our work there, we headed back to Tracy, California, where we stayed and helped the ministry as we waited upon the Lord.

A few months later, we drove down to Oceanside for a job interview. As we approached East Los Angeles, we faced a very difficult and dangerous situation. God protected us and provided help in the nick of time. We arrived safely. A few weeks later, I received a job offer, and we decided to make San Diego our new home. We hitched up our trailer, said our goodbyes to family, and headed down south the following weekend. On our way, we visited my sister in Clovis and spent the night there. "The fog is thick. Are you sure you need to leave today?" my sister asked.

"Yes. I start work on Monday," I replied. There was very little visibility, but we slowly continued driving. We were approaching

Kingsburg, when I slammed on the brakes, barely missing the car ahead. We could hear the sirens of the rescue vehicles attempting to get to the location. We later saw on the news that it was a forty-car pileup. Grateful that God had protected us, we continued our journey.

After a few places, we eventually settled into an RV park in San Ysidro to be close to the church we attended. Our bishop offered Lupito a pastorship. We didn't feel it was God's will at the time and turned it down. Lupito was appointed to be a district evangelist. This opened doors to minister to the churches in the area and in Mexico. God granted me my dream job of working for the San Diego School District as a secretary to an elementary principal. Finally, we had found our new home.

Eight months later, however, because of a family emergency, we quit our jobs and moved up north to Clovis. As soon as we could, we were able to move into a home, and God granted me a job working for Clovis Unified. It still was not totally evident where we would place down roots. All we knew was that we had been obedient to His original call and we had sowed seeds of the Gospel in fertile fields. Soon, we would cry out to God in an upcoming journey through a hot and barren land.

Six

Journey through the Desert

Will reap in due season if we do not give up.
—Galatians 6:9

It was a very hot summer day that last Saturday of June 2001, and I was packing for our upcoming trip to Colorado Springs. Lupito's good friend Bishop Chavarria had invited us to minister to the churches under his supervision, and we had planned to leave that following Monday. I could hear Lupito on the phone with another good friend, Bishop Rodriguez from Canoga Park.

He hung up and called out to me. "Hon, the bishop wants us to minister in his church. Why don't we just leave tomorrow to Colorado and stop there on our way?" I knew how much my husband loved and admired his friend, and I agreed that it was a good plan. I had no idea then how invaluable it would be to visit this old friend. His anointed prayer over us would be essential.

Sunday morning, my husband, Victoria, and I got into our small red 1980 Datsun car and headed out of Clovis toward Los

Angeles. We had reached Delano when we noticed that the car was overheating. We were not concerned as it was a very hot day and perhaps the car only needed to cool off. Maybe it just needed water. Lupito put in the water, and we were back on the road. We still had another two hours to go.

The car ran smoothly until we began climbing the steep Grapevine Mountains. The temperature gauge of our four-cylinder car began to rise. "I better pull off and let the car cool down," Lupito said.

I glanced back at my little Victoria. She smiled widely at me. "You know what to do my little one!" I said, as we both lifted our hands toward heaven and prayed.

The car continued to overheat. "I honestly don't know what's the problem," Lupito said. Thankfully, when we began the descent, the car worked like a gem, and we arrived safe and sound in Canoga Park.

After the church service, the bishop noticed our car and exclaimed, "Lupito, you're planning on driving that small thing to Colorado?"

"Yes," Lupito responded. With his hands on our heads, the bishop, earnestly prayed, "Lord, watch over your servants as they travel through rough terrains on their way to Colorado!" The effectual fervent prayer of a righteous man availeth much.

We said our goodbyes and drove off toward Rancho Cucamonga, where we spent the night. Monday morning, we got on the road very early as we needed to be in Colorado Springs by Tuesday, 7:00 p.m. The weather was pleasant, and the car drove great. Two hours later, however, the car began overheating again, and we pulled off in Baker. We noticed the city landmark—a very tall temperature gauge. The weather was 125 degrees! It was hot, and so was our car. We all cooled off for a bit in Baker.

We decided to continue our journey and began the sixteen-mile climb to the next city, Primm, Nevada. The car refused to go beyond a small tree on the side of the road. There, we refreshed for a bit, and Lupito attempted to continue uphill, but the road was just too steep. Lupito decided to return to Baker.

After totally cooling down, we attempted the climb again. I looked back at my little five-year-old, surrounded by her favorite stuffed animals and smiled. My little Victoria rarely, if ever, complained on our journeys.

"Say hi to Pretty, Mom," Victoria said as she waved her little stuffed dog's arm.

"Hi, Pretty," I replied.

"Hi, Victoria's mom," she said in a squeaky voice. We both smiled. We had traveled only two miles, when the car began overheating. "Hon, we need to go back down to Baker."

In Baker, Lupito popped open the hood and attempted to figure out the problem as Victoria and I refreshed ourselves in an A&W restaurant. We were on a limited income, didn't have a major credit card, and there were no available mechanic shops. In our almost ten years of marriage, we had been on many faith-based journeys, and we never lost hope in God. Lupito was usually the one who never gave up. This time, however, I noticed a look of total defeat on his countenance. I believed he was about to give up.

Looking at my little Victoria, I said, "Mija, open your Bible and point your finger to any scripture. I need to hear from the Lord *right now.*"

Victoria happily took out her little Bible from her colorful backpack and opened it. She pointed to the first verse that her eyes fell upon. "Here, Mama," she said, looking expectantly at me.

As I read it, my smile widened: Matthew 4:1—And the Lord was led up to the wilderness to be tempted by the devil. "This is it, mija! The answer. This is just a test we are going through. God will take care of us. We need to tell Papa!"

We could see Lupito coming our way. He pulled open the restaurant door and approached us. Before he could even say a word, I spoke. "Honey, we're going to be OK. This is just a test. I don't know how, but we will get to Colorado." He looked at both of us, somewhat confused. Victoria was smiling happily. I then shared the verse.

"Si, Papa," Victoria beamed. She felt so proud that God had used her this time.

Lupito replied, "I had completely given up. I'm so glad God spoke to you, hon."

As we got back into our Datsun, I said, "Hon, a man told me that if we turn the heater on, the car will not overheat."

"OK, let's do it!" Lupito said. With the heater on and pillows protecting my and Victoria's feet, we happily began our journey up the steep highway toward Nevada. As we neared the same small tree, the temperature gauge rose higher than ever, and the car turned off. We pulled off to let the car cool down, and once the car started up again, we returned to Baker.

Still believing that this was a test of our faith, I said, "OK, let's go back." One way or another, I absolutely knew that God was going to get us to Colorado. "Hon, I saw a U-Haul truck when we entered Baker. Maybe we can rent one."

"OK, let's go check it out!" Lupito replied. "There it is!" It turned out to be just an old truck, covered with spider webs, on an abandoned property.

Not giving up, I said, "Honey, maybe we can find a car rental in Las Vegas—one that accepts debit cards."

We noticed the phone booth across the street. I was glad there was an address book attached to it, and I looked up car rentals. To my dismay, the pages were torn out! There was only a half page that said "Dollar-Rent-A-Car." All I could see was 1-800. Taking a guess, I decided to dial 1-800-rentcar. I dialed 1-800-736-8227.

"Hello, Rent-A-Car, can I help you?" a woman said. I felt relieved when I heard her voice and even more so when she told me that they took debit cards and there would be a car available at twelve midnight. (The time was 5:30 p.m.) She told me that she would need to put a hold on my debit card. This presented a problem as we had withdrawn all our funds prior to the trip, and I now needed to redeposit $300.

We drove to the ARCO gas station a block away. Earlier, I had noticed there was an ATM machine there. As I walked toward it, I saw the sign "No Deposits" and temporarily felt disillusioned. I decided to check our account balance even though I knew that the balance should be zero. *Please, God. Let there be funds available.* To my big surprise, there was $700. "Hon, there's $700! I'm not sure why, and I can't even call the bank." (It was after work hours). We called back and the agency reserved the car.

Now we needed to find a way to get to Las Vegas, Nevada, from Baker. Recalling a casino bus that drove in hours earlier,

Lupito asked the Arco manager about transportation to Nevada. He informed us that there would be another bus coming in at 7:00 p.m. He also gave us permission to park our car on the property for a week.

Grateful that we at least found a way to get to Nevada, where a car was waiting for us, we still had to figure out how to get to the airport. We kept ourselves in a prayerful attitude because we knew that God was in complete control. God knew we needed some rest before ministering in Colorado Springs at 7:00 p.m. the next day. God knew that the time frame of things at the present would not work out. God was about to work everything to His perfection.

It was 6:00 p.m. when a car drove up next to us and parked. Lupito noticed the two young men as they got out of their car and headed inside the market. "Hon, I'll be right back." He walked their way and quickly struck up a conversation with them. They spoke Spanish only. A few minutes later, Lupito returned and said, "Hon, those two men have offered to take us to the airport rental place for the price of a bus ticket. What do you think?" I looked at them. They appeared to be kind, honest young men. They had only stopped for a snack before getting back on the road toward Las Vegas. If we left now, we would save an hour and not have to find a way from the strip to the airport. I had no doubt that we were under God's protection.

Trusting God, we loaded our luggage into their car. We had to leave Victoria's stuffed animals. "Don't worry, mija. They'll be there when we come back." As we headed toward Nevada, we noticed the small tree that we had not been able to pass. Their car worked just fine. A few minutes later, a sandstorm picked up. We could barely see. After a while, the winds subsided, and now, there was a downpour. Will the young men throw us out like Jonah? It felt like the enemy was mad that we were passing the test. After twenty minutes or so, the rain stopped, and the sun shone brightly. It felt like it was beating upon the car with all its strength. I immediately thought of Jesus's three temptations that He faced when he went up to the wilderness to be tested. Shortly after, the weather seemed to calm down. The two young men found their voices and commented that they had never experienced anything like that. As promised, they took us directly to the Las Vegas airport.

Lupito thanked the young men as I jumped off and walked over to the agency. The young men helped him with our luggage but refused to leave until they knew we were safe. The agent informed me that their car would be returned at twelve midnight. It was only 8:00 p.m. She offered to see if by chance it was returned early and walked outside. She returned, looking quite surprised. "It looks like it's been returned already." God knew we could not afford to lose those precious four hours. We got back on the road, rested for four hours, and arrived in Colorado Springs at 7:00 p.m. sharp. God's anointing was upon us as we ministered that first evening.

After church, we enjoyed a good dinner with Bishop Chavarria and family. As we got ready to leave, the bishop's son said, "Wait, Dad!" He put his quarter in the Denny's claw machine. "Maybe I'll win this time." *He had never won.* "Dad, I got one!" he yelled. He offered the colorful bear to Victoria. "Here, Victoria." She shyly thanked him as she hugged her new little bear. She was missing all her little friends she had left in our parked Datsun. The Lord remembered her. We spent the

next seven days ministering, counseling, encouraging, and making new friends. God blessed us immeasurably.

We returned to the Arco Gas Station in Baker and found the Datsun just as we had left it. Victoria and I followed Lupito in the rental. The car overheated again. Victoria and I watched Lupito pop open the hood. A few minutes later, he slammed the hood down. With a big smile and a thumbs-up, Lupito yelled. "It won't overheat anymore, hon. I figured out the problem. From that moment on, the Datsun did not overheat.

Could God have purposely closed Lupito's mind to the problem, forcing us to consider taking a rental? Perhaps a twenty-year-old, four-cylinder car would have not made the steep climbs and rough terrains we faced as we traveled Nevada, Utah, and Colorado. And what was the explanation for the $700 bank error that was corrected after seven days? We continued to see God's hand as we sowed the seed of the Gospel. Four months later, when we traveled to Houston, Texas, for another event, God moved miraculously. We depended on Him in these faith-based journeys. When Lupito got a permanent job in Clovis, however, we felt we could now settle down and live in comfort. Soon, we were to find out that this was not to be the case.

Seven

Delivered from Death

In the shadow of His Hand hath He hid me.
—Isaiah 49:2

"Today, I'm going to help Kevin overcome his fear of heights," Lupito said as he jumped in his brown Ford truck. *How did he plan to do that?* I wondered.

"Honey, have an amazing day. Love you!!" I said as I waved goodbye to him. Lupito was so happy that he had gotten a steady job working for the City of Clovis. "Love you!" Lupito shouted as he drove off, heading toward the Clovis Landfill on Auberry Road. It was November 6, 2002, a day I will always remember.

Six hours later, I headed back home from work. As I walked into our Beverly Street home, I heard the phone ringing. I hurried inside and answered the phone. "Hello?"

"Hi, this is Liz from the City of Clovis. Is this Mrs. Bravo?"

"Yes." She hesitated and then spoke. "The ambulance is taking your husband to the hospital right now. He fell from the conveyor belt. I'm sorry."

Trying to calm myself, I quickly got in the car and went to pick up my son and daughter from school. "Please pray for Dad. Something happened at work!" I anxiously told them as I rushed to the hospital.

When I arrived, I noticed an ambulance arriving at the same time. I looked at the man on the bed. Lupito! He was covered with blood, and the paramedics were running to an elevator. "Stay here!" I told my kids as I ran toward the elevator. I went in and looked at Lupito. His eyes were closed. "Honey, I'm here," I quietly said as I silently stood in a corner. As soon as the elevator opened, they pointed to a waiting room as they ran through the double doors leading toward surgery. As the word got out about my husband, people began pouring into that large waiting room. Family members, church members, coworkers in unity began praying for God's mercy. Unanswered questions remained in our minds as we waited. How bad was the fall? Was there a spinal cord injury? If he lived, would he be a paraplegic? Did he have a brain injury? As we waited the long hours, I was able to piece together what had happened.

The electric tumbler at the landfill had stopped working because of overload. Everyone got busy cleaning it. Meanwhile, Lupito decided to clean the conveyor belt as well. He climbed to the top to remove trash. He heard a sound and felt movement under his feet. His coworker had pressed the wrong button and started the conveyor belt. Having nothing to grab on to, Lupito fell at least forty feet. At that very moment, the scooper operator was rushing in to collect trash and barely had time to stop. It didn't prevent Bravo (as they called him) from hitting a corner of that metal scooper, crushing his ribs. He ended up on the rocky ground, unable to breathe.

Kevin, Lupito's coworker and friend, could not believe what he was witnessing. This was the very day that Bravo said he would help him get over his fear of heights. A paramedic in training lifted Bravo to help him breathe. As they waited for the ambulance, an intimate conversation took place between Lupito and his God.

Lupito: *Lord, here I am.*

God: No.

Then take this pain away.

God: No.

Then what?

God: Take the pain. Play dead.

It was then that Lupito surrendered to the pain that riveted his whole body.

As we anxiously waited in the hospital, I overheard Lupito's boss. "Was there a lockout on Bravo's machine?"

Supervisor Butch answered, "No." I realized then that safety procedures were broken. The lockout would have prevented someone from accidentally turning on the conveyor.

We had been waiting for six hours when a doctor approached me. "Mrs. Bravo?"

"Yes?"

"I'm the orthopedic doctor. I reattached your husband's wrist to his right hand. The surgeon performed a laparotomy due to Mr. Bravo's internal bleeding. The internal bleeding did not stop, however, forcing the doctor to reopen him. He will be coming out soon to talk to you."

At around 10:00 p.m., a surgeon walked into the waiting room. "Mrs. Bravo? The surgery was successful ..." A sigh of relief was heard in the room. "And he will be taken to intensive care now where we will continue to monitor his situation." He continued, "Mr. Bravo broke eleven ribs, punctured his lungs, wounded his kidneys and pancreas, and slivered his liver. He had severe internal bleeding. He is not out of danger." Thanking the surgeon, Pastor Roy gathered everyone in a circle. We thanked the Lord for guiding the surgeon's hands and uplifted my husband in prayer.

The following morning, a doctor reviewed Lupito's medical records as Lupito's brother Rick and I waited by the bedside. We stood watching him. He looked up and said, "No one falls fifty feet and lives to talk about it."

Rick and I looked at each other, "Fifty feet?" Up until that moment, we never knew how high the fall was from.

The doctor asked, "Is he a diabetic?"

"No," I responded.

"Well, he is now. We are giving him insulin."

I spent my days at the hospital. Most of the time, Lupito was in an induced coma and unable to breathe on his own. We sang his favorite songs, and ministers came daily to say prayers over him. One day, as we stood by his bed, he lifted two fingers up. Juan, my brother-in-law, and I got very excited to see this. "What's he trying to say?" I said to Juan. We tried to guess. "It's a 2 ... No, it's a V! He wants Victoria!" Juan went to sneak her in. "Be very quiet, Victoria. Your dad wants you."

"OK, Tio." Victoria responded, displaying the most beautiful smile. She was going to see Papa. Maybe she could sing "Tomorrow," the song she had been singing to Papa before the accident. When she arrived at his bedside, her tears gushed out. "Hi, Papa. I miss you so much." Papa touched her little hand.

A few seconds later, a nurse came over. "She can't be here!" she sternly said.

"Yes, we're sorry," Juan said as he quickly ushered little Victoria out. Lupito had gotten his wish.

Lupito was taken off the ventilator, and he was being weaned off the morphine. I was happy he could talk now. I greeted him, and he anxiously spoke. I could barely hear him, so I got very close to listen. "Leave the truck here. I'm going to escape," he said. *What?* "Put cream on your face." He continued. *Was my face that dry?* "Don't dye your hair."

"Hon, I responded, I haven't dyed my hair." I was surprised at what he was saying. "Good, because everyone here is dyeing their hair. Also, there are a lot of termites here," Lupito stressed.

I felt sad and confused. "OK, hon," I responded, "I'll be right back." I walked out of the IC unit and walked toward the waiting room.

Dr. Montes, Lupito's doctor, was coming around the corner and noticed my worried look. Before I could say anything, he said, "Do not worry, Mrs. Bravo. Your husband is experiencing hallucinations because of morphine withdrawal. It's normal. It will wear off."

That night, Lupito got out of control and insisted they release him. He told the nurses that he was going to have his brother Dario arrest them for keeping him there against his will. It had been a difficult night. They had to sedate him.

That next day, I was told that Lupito had pneumonia. The doctors had always been concerned about this and had even put him in a rotation bed to avoid any fluid buildup. This would seriously complicate matters. I was grateful for the friends and family who kept me company in the waiting room and prayed with me. An hour later, a nurse informed me that my mom was on the courtesy phone at the nurse's station. "Hi, Mom."

"Hola, Betty. Como esta Lupe?"

"He's the same, Mom." I decided to unburden my heart. "I just found out that he has pneumonia, Mom."

My mom became silent. Very quietly, as though talking to herself, she said, "And many have died from that, especially in his fragile condition."

Her words filled me with dread. "Mom!" I had been in a spiritual realm of faith the whole time, not once believing that God would take my husband away. Our church members prayed and fasted for his recovery. When I returned to the waiting room and sat down, my sister-in-law Martha, sensing despair in my spirit, put her arms around me. Tears began flowing down my cheeks. Everyone in the room became quiet. Gaining renewed strength and hope at that very moment, I wiped my tears. I truly believed God still had a purpose on this earth for Lupito.

As November came to an end, I noticed Lupito's health seemed to be improving. One day, they wheeled him out of the IC unit to a regular hospital room. I felt so relieved. From the hospital, he was placed in a rehabilitation hospital. God had performed a miracle. When the doctor released him to go home, I felt such joy in my soul. The day I wheeled him into our church, the members stood and applauded him as I wheeled him to share words with the congregation. They were witnessing a miracle that day. God had answered all our prayers.

A year after the accident, we were walking toward the entrance of Walmart in Clovis, when we saw a paraplegic ministering from his wheelchair. He was playing a hands-free harmonica and speaking about God from a microphone attached to his chair. As we got closer, we recognized the man. It was our old friend John, the owner of a towing company. He had come to our rescue a few times when we needed help with our fifth wheel trailer. We learned that after a visit to see Lupito in the hospital, he was called to tow a vehicle. On his way there, he had a major accident that paralyzed him from the neck down. It was hard to see John like this. He was a tall, 6'4" Caucasian man in his early fifties, who looked like Kenny Rogers. He had a successful business and a very sweet, kind wife. John lost everything this world offered, but he never lost his love and devotion to God.

Reflecting on our lives, I concluded that no matter what happens, God must always be first. It humbled us to see John.

That could have been Lupito, but God spared his life on the sixth day of November. We had seen the operation of God's hand upon our lives once. A year had passed, and I could see that my husband had regained all his strength and seemed ready to mount up with wings like an eagle.

One experience will always be prominent is when
my dad almost died. He fell forty feet onto a tractor's
shovel teeth thing. I remember the day I was called
out of class. He was in a horrible condition. I was
very quiet. My mom was worried about me, but
really, I was fine. I wasn't worried about my dad. I
knew that the Lord was going to help him recover,
and sure enough he is a walking miracle. I believe
this just reinstilled my faith in God. I know that
all things work for the good of those who love
God and are called according to His purpose. This
has been made evident all throughout my life.
—Victoria

Eight

I Think Another Testimony's Coming On

BY VICTORIA ANGELICA BRAVO (NOW SOTO)
(COPIED FROM HER SCHOOL JOURNAL 2010)

Since my birth, I've gone on many trips with my parents, promoting my mother's recordings and attending many church events. Many of these trips were accomplished with very little finance and a lot of faith. I will never forget, however, one of these trips where it appeared that we would not have to go on faith once again as we had done so many times in the past.

It all began on November 23, 2003. My mom was happy because finally, we had a good vehicle and even extra money for our trip to Anaheim, California, that day. This time, my mom wanted to go like normal people do, like her sister, she told my dad. Just to be totally on the safe side, she had my dad take our family van to the mechanics to make sure everything was OK prior to heading out of Clovis that day.

That day, everything was going just great. As we approached Grapevine Mountain in Bakersfield, my mom was so relaxed that she decided to begin a journal about all our previous trips that we had taken, which ended up all being testimonies of God's greatness and His intervention in helping us to get to our destination. This time was different, though, as Mom felt totally secure that we would have absolutely no transportation troubles getting to our National Church Convention. She even had $400 to spend. We did not even pray as we climbed up the Grapevine this time as had been customary in all our other trips. As we were approaching the top of the mountain, the van began to make a horrible noise. I was only five years old at the time, and immediately, the first words out of my mouth were "I think another testimony's coming on." I could see that my mom's joy immediately turned to worry. Mom slowly put her journal away and grabbed her Bible instead. She opened it up to the first verse that her eyes fell on and read it. It was Psalm 119:71–72 that said, "It was good for me to be afflicted so that I might learn your decrees. The law from your mouth is more precious to me than thousands of pieces of silver and gold." I could see that my mom's attitude changed. She became more prayerful and repentant because she felt that God was telling her that she had failed to put Him in first place for this trip as had been done all our lives. We waited on the side of the highway for some help.

My dad called everyone, but no one was home. Finally, my mom had to agree, reluctantly, to hand over her spending money to call a tow truck and to cover other expenses. When the tow truck driver came, my mom asked my dad whether we would stay in the van as we were towed up the Grapevine to the nearest gas station. My dad said that surely that would not be the case. However, the tow truck driver told us to stay in the van, and there we were being towed as we sat in our van. I thought it was the coolest thing, but my mom and dad were appalled and nervous that the van might slip off the truck. Also, it was quite embarrassing because the people could see us sitting in the van on the back of the tow truck.

To make this long story short, in the end, we did go to the convention. With the help of a stranger (someone who needed gas to get to Fresno), two uncles (Benjamin and Rick), a very old truck, and God, of course, we were able to go to the national convention after all. Although my mom no longer had her $400 spending money and our nice van, we still enjoyed the trip and knew once again that God was in control. We were humbler and more dependent upon God once again, and our attitudes were more focused upon His purpose in our lives. We had a great time at the conventions. We sold many tapes, and once again, we were able to conquer the obstacles that we faced. I was my same old happy self, full of expectation of fun things to continue to happen to our family. When we got home, we thanked God for being there with us and asked Him for forgiveness for leaving Him out of the picture, when He had always been there for us in every other journey until we forgot about Him.

My reflection after reading Victoria's school report:
On this journey, I had placed my "trust on chariots" (Psalm 20:7) and not on God. My relationship with Him was so close that He

let me know that I had displeased Him. The following year, we would experience one of the most rewarding journeys of our lives. This time, God would give me a vision of the future.

Nine

Hebrews 11:11-
Vision of the Future

He that goeth forth and weeping, bearing
precious seed, shall doubtless come again with
rejoicing, bringing his sheaves with him.
—Psalm 126:6

It was a cold November evening when the call came. "Hello?" Lupito answered. We had just finished dinner. After speaking to someone, Lupito hung up. He appeared so excited. "Hon! It was Bishop Castro. He's offering us a pastorship!"

"He is?" I was taken aback. A year before, Lupito almost died. And now, he would soon be a pastor? "Where?" I asked.

"Avenal."

"Avenal? Where's that?"

"I don't really know," Lupito answered.

"I think it's down the 5 somewhere. Bishop said the church is on Skyline Boulevard."

I quickly grabbed an area map. "Let's look it up. There it is. Skyline is Avenal's major street. It's a little more than an hour down south."

Lupito said, "It's not that far. Let's go check it out!"

Fifteen minutes later, we were on the 41, heading southwest toward Avenal. We traveled a little over an hour. The last five miles, we climbed up some hills parallel to Interstate 5 and descended into a small, isolated town. We found the church right away and parked in front of a light-green stucco building and peeked inside its two front windows. "I love it! There's even a big grocery store across the street. It's in a prime area," I commented. We felt great peace when we returned to Clovis. God had a new journey ahead for us.

The bishop installed Lupito as the pastor. We commuted three times a week from Clovis and spent many hours connecting with people and planting the seeds of the Gospel in the ground of Avenal. We relocated to Avenal and temporarily lived in our fifth-wheel trailer on the church property. We had many revivals and outreach events. "Honey, I commented one day, it's been six months since the bishop installed us, and no one has asked for the baptism."

"I know," Lupito replied. "I've been wondering if the ground is fertile."

About a week later, I began to see the numbers 11 11. "Hon, I don't understand, but I am constantly seeing the numbers 11 11 everywhere—I'm wondering if God is trying to warn us or something," I told my husband one day.

Two days later, I was in a deep sleep when I heard "*11 11.*" At first it sounded like a gentle whisper. I thought I was dreaming "*11*

11." The voice gradually got louder. Finally, it got so loud that I woke up. *"Hebrews 11: 11!"* It was no longer a whisper. Something, someone was yelling a Bible scripture into my ear! I jumped up, waking up Lupito. "Something just happened right now. I heard a loud voice. You didn't hear it?"

Lupito responded, "No."

"God just spoke. Remember how I kept seeing the numbers 11 11 everywhere?"

Lupito nodded.

"Well, I think I know the meaning now. It's a scripture."

Lupito quickly grabbed his old Reina Valera Bible he kept by his bedside.

Gently touching his hand, I stopped him. "Wait, hon, not now. Let's read it at the altar in the morning. This is powerful, and I want to give it the reverence it deserves." We both laid our heads back down on the pillow and tried to get in a few more hours of sleep.

That morning, we quickly got dressed and walked into the church. We knelt at the altar and prayed to God. We then reverently opened the Bible to Hebrews 11:11, and this is what we read: "And by faith even Sarah, who was past childbearing age, was enabled to bear children because she considered him faithful who had made the promise." The revelation hit me immediately. "Hon, I understand what God is telling us! There will be baptisms in Avenal! Babies will be born soon. The ground is fertile." This scripture was perfect. I, like Sarah, had struggled giving birth until the Lord blessed me with my two children. And Lupito, like Abraham, was as good as dead when he fell forty feet the year before. He was a walking miracle. Further, it was the story of Abraham and Sarah that we had been listening to on the radio when we made the decision to leave everything and obeyed His call upon our lives. There couldn't have been a more perfect verse.

Three months later, we had our first baptism. It was exactly nine months from the day we were installed as the pastor. In a year, twenty-two souls (11 plus 11) received the Lord as their savior. A new mission church was even planted in Lemoore, a neighboring city. There was fruit in a supposed barren land. There was even a dream I had seven years earlier about Avenal. God always had a purpose for my husband and me in that city.

After third grade, my dad got a pastorship in Avenal, California. I was sad to be moving from my Clovis church. It was an amazing experience helping a mission grow into a church. I learned many things about how to deal with people. I got to be part of testimony in which the Lord told my mom in a dream Hebrews 11:11, practically yelling it in her ear. The significance in this verse is that my parents considered themselves like Abraham and Sarah of the Bible. Abraham was called out of his homeland just like my parents were called out by faith to leave Stockton. My mom has had at least three miscarriages, considering herself barren like Sarah. Therefore, Josh and I are considered miracle children. The scripture was a promise for growth in the mission church of Avenal, and sure enough, there were twenty-two baptisms by the end of that year. The seed was planted, and it flourished.

—Victoria's school report

A dream comes to pass

The pastor's wife, Teresa, of the Avenal Assembly of God church invited me to speak at their Christmas gathering. I asked my sister to pray for me. "I want God to use me!"

"Call me after!" she said. "I want to know how it went!" I felt God's presence as I spoke that evening. Right before dismissal, Teresa asked if I could play the piano for the ladies. "Of course!" I said as I got up and walked to an old upright piano I had noticed in the corner. Teresa invited all the ladies, and they formed a crescent moon behind me and beautifully sang the song "Silent Night."

Later that night, I called my sister. "Margaret, they received the message. It was odd though. Even though their own band had been playing, Teresa asked me to play for the ladies. Thankfully, there was an upright piano there."

My sister was silent for a moment. "Betty?" she said.

"What?" I replied.

"Don't you remember?" She continued, "The dream about the piano some years ago?"

I thought for a moment, and then it hit me. "Oh my! That's right!" I had forgotten. I could feel God's presence. I was so grateful that I had told my sister about the dream when I had it years earlier. God was going to use her to bring it back to my memory!

The original dream given to me seven years earlier

I walked into a big church building and noticed a large gathering of people from the church organization I belonged to. I admired the beautiful sanctuary. I noticed a small balcony and decided to walk upstairs. Other than an old upright piano against the wall on a red carpeted floor, the place was empty. I sat down to play the piano. I began to hear the word "one" whispered in my ear over and over. *One?* I thought. Maybe it was a song with the number "one" in it, and I placed my thumb on the key of C to begin to play the song that came to my mind, "One, One, One, One Way to God"—a short chorus I had known for many years. A leader of my church organization had composed it. Just as I prepared to play it, a group of women out of nowhere gathered behind me, forming the shape of a crescent moon. Immediately, they began singing before I could start playing the song. The song they were singing with such harmony and beauty was called "There's Room at the Cross for You." I had never heard it sung with such an anointing. When the women got to the part in the song that said, "Though millions have come, there's still room for one," the word "one" was stretched out and sung with such an amazing melodious harmony. This was the song that God had wanted me to play! I concluded. That was the "one" that was being repeated in my mind. God was speaking to me through this song and the group of women. The women appeared to be from an Assembly of God organization—whose doctrine was different from mine. The love that flowed as they sang was strong, and the message that they delivered to me through that song was so powerful. While the other song I was about to play emphasized there was only one way to God, this song emphasized God's merciful grace and the room for one.

No doubt, the hand of God continued to move upon our lives. He seemed to always have a plan for us. A few years later, we would once again experience dreams and incidents that would reveal that God was continually watching over us. It all started when someone decided to steal our van.

Ten

Robbed at Home and in Rome

Therefore, let us not sleep, as others do,
but let us watch and be sober.
—1 Thessalonians 5:6

My cell phone rang. It was Lupito. I wondered why he was calling instead of just coming into the house. "Honey, why did you just take off like that? You didn't even say bye."

Lupito asked. "Huh? What are you talking about? I'm in the house. I haven't left yet."

I replied, confused by his question.

Lupito yelled, "Nos robaron!" and quickly hung up. I ran outside just in time to see Lupito making a U-turn with his truck. I noticed our Nissan Quest van was gone. "I'm going to find them! Call the police!"

Shortly afterward, Lupito returned. "They got away!" He explained. "A lady jumped in our van while I was cleaning out my truck. I looked, but I thought it was you. I was concerned though, so I kept looking and noticed that she stopped down the street and picked up two guys. At first, I thought it was Joshua and a friend. But it just didn't feel right, so I called you."

Three days later, the police found the car abandoned in an orchard. It was returned to us, but Lupito didn't feel good about the van anymore and decided to sell it. The sad thing was that Victoria's photo album and key chain collection of all her travels were not returned—treasures that could not be replaced.

With the money from the sale of the van, we paid for a cruise to Europe. It was on the *Voyager of the Seas*, which would leave from the port of Barcelona in November of that year.

One night, both Lupito and I awoke out of our sleep in the middle of the night, disturbed by dreams. My dream was beautiful; Lupito's dream was a nightmare. In my dream, I had walked out of our bedroom, with my hands lifted. I was worshipping God with my hands lifted as I walked our long winding hallway toward a treasure that was waiting for me at the front door of our home. Lupito, in his dream, found himself outside the house. He was pounding on the front door, calling for me to let him in. There was a huge dark, ominous cloud headed his way. It felt evil, and the front door was locked. These dreams took place exactly eleven days before our eleven-hour plane trip for our eleven-day vacation. We wondered if the dream was a warning about our impending trip to Europe.

The evening before our flight, we had a visitor. We heard loud singing outside. "Do you hear the singing?" I told Lupito. I peeked outside and saw my brother's golden Plymouth Voyager van in front. "It's Benjie!" I said as I opened the door.

The whole family was singing loudly "O Happy Day!"

"Come inside!" I said laughing. Benjie and the family walked in. "We thought we'd give you a happy send-off song to Europe!" We had a very pleasant evening with my brother and family.

That next morning, we boarded the plane in San Francisco. Eleven hours later, we arrived in Paris and boarded another plane to Spain. Two hours later, we arrived. Two kind Spaniards helped us lift our heavy luggage onto the train and pointed us in the direction of Las Ramblas, our destination. Once we got off the train, another stranger happened to be going in the direction of our hotel and walked with us. We checked in and decided to go look for someplace to eat dinner. There was a beautiful cathedral in front. As we approached it, we noticed a group of people playing guitars. The song they were singing was "O Happy Day!" The very song that had been our send-off in California was our welcoming song in Spain. We believed God was in control of this trip.

Three days later, we boarded the beautiful Royal Caribbean Cruise ship. The ship was to take us to Nice, Pisa, Sicily, Palermo, Pompeii, Rome.

One morning, as the ship was approaching Rome, we were awakened around 5:00 a.m. by the sound of a text message. I certainly did not expect to have cell phone service in the middle of the Mediterranean Sea. The time on my cell phone said 11:11—a random time zone that pertained to neither Europe nor the USA. It was a nice message from Benjie. "It's odd that this message came through," I told Lupito. "And look at the time, hon." We both thought it was strange and wondered if God was sending a message our way. Since we were now fully awake, we looked out from our balcony. We saw dark clouds slowly moving across the sky.

"I think there's going to be a downpour in Rome," Lupito said. "Those clouds remind me of the clouds in my dream." As we continued to watch, we noticed the sun began to peek through the clouds. Gradually, the sky became clear and beautiful.

"I think we're going to have great weather!" I commented.

After breakfast, we boarded a tour bus headed toward the Roman Colosseum. The tour guide warned us to watch out for the Romani (gypsies). She told us to guard our valuables. We arrived, and just as we got ready to get off the bus, Victoria exclaimed loudly, "Mom! All my pictures are being deleted!" Our twelve-year-old had been taking pictures with her little camera of our many journeys. She was unable to stop the deletion. Eight hundred pictures gone just like that! This caused us to fall behind, and we were separated from our tourist guide. Victoria rushed to catch the group up, and I raced to catch up with Victoria. Lupito fell behind. I didn't want to lose sight of my daughter, so I didn't look back. I was sure he would catch us up eventually. Since the day we began planning for this European trip, I had looked forward to the day I would stand in front of the Colosseum. I wanted to acknowledge the sacred memory of the saints whose lives were taken there because of their belief in Christ. We were walking up a winding pathway when I noticed a gypsy. I remembered the warning and made sure to walk on the other side of the pathway.

Lupito felt so bad because Victoria had lost valuable photos and was not as alert to his surroundings as he needed to be. To think, just three months earlier, she had lost her valuable photo albums and key chains. A gypsy thief noticed an opportunity when she saw Lupito and approached him. She pointed to her stomach and a sign she was holding. Apparently, she was pregnant and begging for money. As Lupito read the sign, she saw her opportunity. Two other gypsies joined her, and among the three, they stole his wallet. Pulling out his cash, they dropped his wallet and ran. A few men who noticed the situation ran to help Lupito pick up his cards from the wet ground. Lupito had been yelling my name, but I did not hear him. I looked back at the winding pathway and saw him at the top of the steps. "BettyI" he yelled angrily, "Me robaron!" Victoria and I both ran back to join him. At that instant, our dreams—the winding pathway, the gloomy dark clouds, calling out my name, being alone, and the treasure at the end—came to our minds. Victoria had lost precious pictures, and a robbery was committed. It resembled what had happened to us back at home. This time, it was in Rome. As we reflected on our dream and the 11:11 text, we concluded that perhaps it had been a warning, alerting us of what was to happen. There was no doubt that God was always watching out for us on our journeys.

Years later, on a trip to Idaho, we would once again see the hand of God move in our lives. I will never forget this trip. This time, my son Joshua would go with us. It could have been the end of our lives. That is how close we came to death on this journey.

Eleven

God Sends a Ram

...He rewards those who earnestly seek him.
—Hebrews 11:6

"I can't wait to go to Idaho to see my son!" Lupito happily said. We were discussing ways to stretch our budget for the upcoming trip. "How about we stay one night in Meridian at my friend's home?" I asked. "Sounds good." Lupito agreed as he looked out the window at our Nissan Quest van. "We can't afford to rent a car, hon."

"I know," Lupito answered. "Don't worry—our van works fine."

The following weekend, we headed out of San Diego to pick up Joshua in Lemoore. "Hi, Josh!"

"Hi, Mom! Can't wait to see Israel!" I could feel his excitement as he loaded his luggage into the van. We then took off to Clovis to spend the night at my sister's. Early the next morning, we headed north toward Idaho.

In Winnemucca, Nevada, we stopped for an early dinner. "Boy, that KFC was good!" Lupito said.

"Yes!" Joshua and Victoria agreed. "You were starving us, Mom!"

"Well, don't forget my friend Helen said she has a great soup waiting for us."

We got back on the two-lane highway. We had traveled some fifteen miles when we felt a drop in speed. "Not sure what's happening, hon, the van won't go past 20 mph." Lupito started praying, placing his hand on the dashboard. The van seemed to speed up a bit. When he took his hand off, it slowed back down.

"Keep your hand on the dashboard, Dad. Your prayers are being heard," Joshua teased.

"Yes, Papa." Victoria laughed. "Don't move your hand." I was glad they were in a good mood despite our troubles.

We continued to drive forward. The highway became lonelier. There were no gas stations, no mechanic shops, and no phone service. We passed a sign, "Jordan Valley, Oregon, 40 Miles." Night had fallen. The clear sky displayed its magnificent stars, and we saw a few scattered house lights here and there. As we neared a steep mountain ahead, we noticed a campground. It was called Rome Station. "I'm turning in here. Maybe they have a gas pump. We're running out of gas," Lupito said.

We stood in the safety of our van as Lupito got off. He knocked on a cabin door, and a man answered. A moment later, Lupito returned. "He's going to sell us gas from their private pump."

Now with a full tank, Lupito headed toward the exit. He looked toward the left, and seeing no traffic, he prepared to pull out onto the lonely highway. At that very instant, I noticed four headlights coming off the steep mountain. Four? I immediately reacted to the imminent danger and slapped Lupito's arm, forcing him to stop. "Hon, stop! Don't go forward!" Speeding down from the steep mountain were two eighteen-wheelers. It appeared that one was attempting to pass the other and had crossed over to the lane we were entering. Lupito slammed on the brakes, and we launched forward. We were inches from the truck, and the van even shook. We were stunned as we realized how close we had come to death. God had saved us in the nick of time.

Feeling desperate for a place where we could find a motel to sleep and possibly cell phone service, Lupito decided to get back on the road. It was 10:00 p.m. "I'm hoping we can make it to Jordan Valley." The van began to make a loud noise. "I think we lost the transmission," Lupito said. "I need to get back to the campground." As he attempted a U-turn, the van came to a dead stop in the middle of both lanes.

Realizing the danger, I yelled, "We need to get out! We're sitting ducks here." Just as we opened the doors to jump off, Lupito managed to start up the engine. We held our breath as Lupito slowly returned to the campground. God watched over us as we spent that night in our van.

Early the next morning, we attempted to flag down people. Lupito and I decided to explore the campground to see if anyone could help. Lupito's prayer was that God would send someone in a crew-cab truck where all of us, including our luggage, would fit.

A moment later, we heard Joshua yelling, "Mom! Dad! Come quickly!" We went running toward him. A crew-cab Dodge Ram truck driver was driving into the parking lot. Victoria had flagged him down. As Joshua walked toward the driver, he prayed that we would get there soon. He didn't want the man to change his mind because of his disheveled appearance. We approached just as Joshua had started to explain our situation. The man looked at the four of us and said, "OK, get in. I'll give you a lift to Jordan." He introduced himself. His name was John Smith, a retired history teacher.

As he drove up the mountain, the kind middle-aged man said, "This climb is steep and dangerous. There are no shoulders. You would never have made it in your struggling van." He continued, "I'll need to let my employers know what I'm doing." He detoured up a small hill. "Looks like they left without me," he said as he looked for their truck. Driving back toward the main road, he noticed their truck ahead. "One moment. I see where they are. I'll be right back." We watched him as he got off his truck and walked toward a small group of people. They all turned and looked our way. We prayed that they would not stop the kind man from helping us. Mr. Smith returned and jumped in the truck. "No problem. They'll be fine today. I'm free to help you."

As we got back on the road, Joshua spoke. "My parents have a lot of testimonies of being on the road where God has helped them. I'm glad that now I'm experiencing one of their faith-based journeys." I felt so happy to hear those words coming from my son.

Mr. Smith looked at us and said, "I'd love to hear about your journeys." For the next forty minutes, we shared a few stories. Mr. Smith commented, "Boy, I wish my wife was here. She would love to have heard those stories."

When we arrived in Jordan Valley, we thanked Mr. Smith for the ride. "What will you do here?" he asked. "It's a small town."

"Don't worry. At least there's phone service. We'll figure it out," Lupito answered.

Mr. Smith was quiet, and then he said, "I will take you to Boise."

We protested, "It's almost two hours away!"

He continued, "I'll feel much better leaving you there. At least you'll be able to rent a car there."

Back on the road again, we continued our wonderful conversation about the greatness of God. The trip didn't feel long at all, and soon we saw that we had arrived in Boise. Mr. Smith headed straight to the first car rental he found.

"Thank you, so much," we said as we headed inside the building.

"I'll wait here to make sure you're all OK."

We approached the counter. "We'd like to rent a car," I told a woman at the counter.

"OK," she said, "I'll just need a major credit card."

"Can you take a debit card?" I asked.

"I'm so sorry, but we cannot."

I stood there for a minute when we saw Mr. Smith heading our way. "Are you OK?" he asked. We told him that we needed to find a place that accepted debit cards. He walked to the front counter. "I'd like to rent the car, please," he said. We waited, amazed that he would do that for us.

Ten minutes later, we loaded our luggage into our rental. As we prepared to leave, Lupito offered money to Mr. Smith. "Please let us repay you for your gas at least."

"No," he replied. "I want God's blessings." We said our goodbyes and promised to return the rental the following day.

Time was running out because we needed to be in Burley by 3:00 p.m. that day.

The family event was beautiful, and we were so grateful that we had made it. Aware that we still needed to find a way back to California, Lupito reached out to a few that evening, but no help was found. The following morning, we drove to Twin Falls to return the rental. "Hon," I said, "what if we can't rent a car? Then what?" We walked over to the Budget rental counter. "Hello," I said. "We're returning our rental. Is it possible to rent this car to California with our debit card?" I waited for her response.

"I'm so sorry, but I cannot extend the rental with a debit card."

"OK, thank you," I told her. "I'll be right back. Hon, now what?" I asked. Lupito looked concerned. We sat in the lobby, quietly trying to figure this out as we silently prayed. We saw the woman come toward us.

"Why don't you just keep the rental and return it in California instead? Call Mr. Smith and see if he is willing for you to keep the rental until then."

"Well, hon, that might be our only option," I said as I looked at Lupito.

"OK, I'll be right back." He went to a corner where he had privacy and called Mr. Smith. A few minutes later, he returned. "Mr. Smith said we can return it in California."

The woman at the counter smiled when she saw us. "We have the permission now," I told her.

"OK," she said. She opened her computer to adjust our rental agreement. "You're taken care of. Have a safe trip!"

We had a very pleasant journey returning home. The following day, we dropped off Joshua in Lemoore and picked up our old

Ford truck that was parked there. We headed to Fresno Airport to return the rental. I had spoken earlier to an agent over the phone to get an estimate of what the anticipated cost would be. He informed me that it would be around $814 since we had driven it from Idaho to California without any previous reservations made. We did not have enough to cover that cost. Lupito reminded me that the Lord would help us and to not worry. "Hello," I said, "I'm just returning our rental." I handed her the original paperwork and the keys.

"Thank you. One moment." She looked up the info. "Well, this is strange," she said as she continued to review the information on her computer screen. "Your bill was manually changed. You are being charged the daily rate of $90 for two days only. The entire cost including taxes and fees is $216."

My smile widened as I quickly took out my debit card and handed it to her. Before giving us a copy of the receipt, she wrote a number on it and handed it to me. I looked at the number: 211. I didn't understand why she had written a number that had represented God's involvement in past journeys of our lives.

Epilogue

When I began to write this book, I found the document that I wrote called "The Plan for Growth," and I was amazed at the wonderful "secrets" about church growth and development. God had given me amazing thoughts that brought hope to my heart. All along, He had always had a plan for me. This realization touched the deepest part of my heart.

As I was traveling through the fertile fields where the asparagus grows in Stockton, God looked down and saw my tears. He knew that my only wish was to serve Him with my whole heart and soul. Since I can remember, I love ministering in song. Since I was very young, my mom would dedicate her precious time to teach me church hymns, in Spanish! My Apa would have me sing duets with him in front of large congregations. I vividly remember the day when I sang at San Quentin State Prison, and my song touched a prisoner's heart. He knelt at the altar as tears rolled down his eyes. I was only fifteen.

I long to be that tree planted by the rivers of water, giving fruit even in my old age, until the Lord calls me home and I return to the ground. The joy of producing fruits of the spirit, the amazement of pollinating and contributing toward the spreading of the Gospel and encouraging fruits in others would be the highest privilege. I was planted in the winter season, like the asparagus, in fertile ground that was nutrient rich and well watered. To now flourish in the courts, with song and thanksgiving was a true joy.

Acknowledgments

We were relaxing in our living room while my husband was talking about the fertile fields of the San Joaquin valley. Lupito was telling Jacob how he noticed the fertile grounds every time we exited French Camp Road to visit my father's grave. Being a sower, Lupito always noticed rich ground. Victoria and I were having our own conversation in the dining room when we heard Lupito say, "It's where the asparagus grows."

Victoria and I looked at each other. "That sounds like a good title for the book, Mom!" Victoria said.

"Yes, I do agree!" It caught our attention. As I considered other titles, I kept going back to it. It felt right. I was raised in the valley, and my love for God and my subsequent faith in Him were cultivated there.

These great faith-based traveling experiences,
the wonderful opportunity of meeting so
many people, and my great relationship
with my awesome family have made me
who I am today. They have taught me to
appreciate life as it comes, and to have high

expectations for myself. I believe I can do
the impossible because I have faith.
—Victoria A. Soto (My daughter Victoria
wrote this in 2010 about our journeys.)

Cuando era una niña...

Mi vida ha sido un gran viaje, desde el día que nací. Es que mi papa ha sido un Evangelista y mi mama una pianista y una cantante y por eso hemos viajado a muchos lugares, aun viviendo en nuestra casa movible a veces. Desde niña, he conocido a mucha gente y muchos lugares. Los lugares en el Estados Unidos han sido Texas Arizona, Oklahoma, Idaho, Utah, Washington, New México, Oregón, Nevada, Kansas, y casi todo California. Los otros países han sido México, España, Francia, y Italia. Además de crecer siempre planeados viajes cada ano, he tenido el gusto de pasar por muchas experiencias con gente, transportación y la naturaleza.

En Europa, vimos a Paris, Barcelona, Roma, Mónaco, Pompeya, Pisa y Sicilia. En Paris, estaba muy frío, pero vimos a la Torre de Eiffel. Nos gustó mucho y conocimos a unos franceses allí. En Barcelona, nos quedamos dos días en un hotel cerca de la famosa Calle de Las Ramblas. Había mucho ruido toda la noche. Había un Starbucks donde tome un chocolate. En Roma, vi al Coliseo, donde trataron de robar a mi Papa, pero no tuvieron éxito. También vimos a la Basílica de San Pedro. En Mónaco visitamos a un Jardín exótico, tan bonito y tomamos muchas fotos. También, miramos al Castillo del Príncipe de Mónaco. Estaba muy limpio todo. En Pisa, miramos la torre lidiada de Pisa, y en

Sicilia, miramos a un cementerio "Las Catacumbas" y conocimos al mercado donde compramos muchos dulces italianos.

Como mi vida hasta este punto se ha tratado de viajar, y conocer a muchos países, gentes y lugares históricos, creo yo que ahora tengo en mi sangre de seguir conociendo a todo el mundo, tomando fotos y conociendo a mucha gente de diversas costumbres. Ha sido un grande placer para mi desde mi niñez viajar con mis padres a tantos lugares.

About the Author

Elizabeth Bravo has devoted her life to church ministry and singing. She and her pastor husband have ministered to over four hundred churches and have pastored two churches. Elizabeth was a three-time presenter at State Migrant Education Conferences. She and Lupito have been married for thirty years and together have two sons, two daughters, two sons-in-law, one daughter-in-law, two grandchildren, and two grand-doggies, Mia and Beaux.

Printed in the United States
by Baker & Taylor Publisher Services

Printed in the United States
by Baker & Taylor Publisher Services